i

ii

THE WISDOM OF
SAM ERVIN

BILL M. WISE

Introduction by Senator Howard H. Baker, Jr.

BALLANTINE BOOKS • NEW YORK

Cover photo by Fred Ward from Black Star

Photo credits : p. i from Wide World Photos ; ii by
Dennis Brack from Black Star ; vi-vii from Wide
World Photos ; viii (top) from Wide World
Photos ; viii (bottom) from Wide World Photos ;
ix (top) by Fred Ward from Black Star ; ix
(bottom) from Wide World Photos ; x (top) by
Fred Ward from Black Star ; x (bottom) by
Dennis Brack from Black Star ; xi (top) from
Wide World Photos ; xi (bottom) from Wide
World Photos ; xii (top) from Wide World
Photos ; xii (bottom) from Wide World Photos ;
xiii from Wide World Photos ; Photos ; xiv-xv
from Wide World Photos ; xvi from Wide World
Photos

E
748
.E93
E7
1973
Dec. 1996

BALLANTINE BOOKS, INC.
201 East 50th Street, New York, N.Y. 10022

Photographs

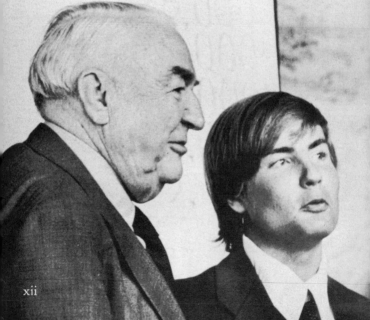

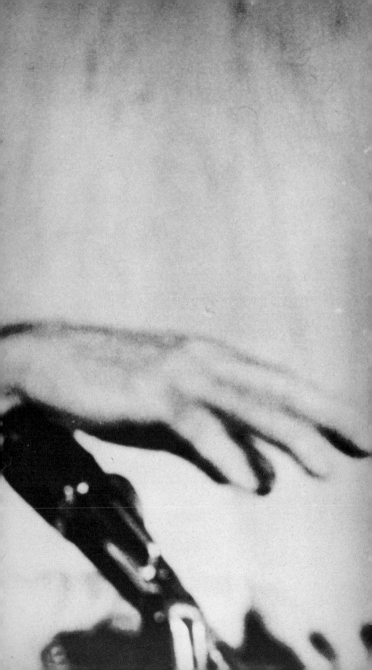

xvi

Work with
Rep Senate —
get illustration

The Wisdom of Sam Ervin

ACKNOWLEDGMENTS

Many thanks to Rufus L. Edmisten, Robert B. Smith, Jr., Hall Smith, Eugene Boyce, Phillip Haire, Lawrence M. Baskir, J. William Heckman, and Gail-Joy Alexander.

CONTENTS

INTRODUCTION

As a neighbor from across the mountains, I feel that I have a good many things in common with the people of North Carolina. Today perhaps the most significant of these sentiments that we share is an abiding affection and respect for their senior senator and my friend, Sam Ervin.

I have known Senator Ervin ever since I came to the Senate seven years ago, and my admiration for him goes back even further. He is a remarkable individual, an effective lawmaker, a brilliant constitutional scholar, and a distinguished orator. On the Senate floor, I have found him to be a valuable ally and a formidable opponent, but always a fair and decent man.

Delightfully blended with these professional qualities are his personal characteristics, his sense of integrity, warm personality, and down-home charm which have captivated Americans throughout our nation and led them to adopt him as their "Uncle Sam."

With his personal demeanor, his knowledge of the law, and his ever-ready supply of North Carolina stories, Sam Ervin is one of the most commanding Committee Chairmen who has ever wielded a gavel.

I have been proud to serve with him as Vice Chairman of the Senate Select Committee on Presidential Campaign Activities. There are inevitable tugs and twists and conflicts between Republicans and Democrats in such a politically charged atmosphere, but he has gone out of his way to try to accommodate our requirements and to be as fair as humanly possible.

Sam is the only man I know who can read the transcript of a telephone conversation and make it sound like the King James Version of the New Testament, or speak on abstract constitutional doctrine and the philosophical writings of the Founding Fathers with such authority that you almost suspect he just rode up from Charlottesville with them in his saddlebags.

When he inevitably reaches the point in a discourse in which he refers to himself as "Just a poor ol' country lawyer from North Carolina," I am motivated to do two things. First, out of reflex action, I put my hand on my wallet, then I gently remind him that while he may consider himself to be just a poor ol' country lawyer, he is also an honors graduate of Harvard Law School.

That's when Chairman Sam raises his magnificent eyebrows, cocks his head, beams his benign smile, and whispers, "Yes, Howard, but nobody can tell it."

SENATOR HOWARD BAKER

Washington, D.C.
August, 1973

birthday Sept 27 t

PREFACE

Samuel James Ervin, Jr., represents the best that Southern conservatism has to offer. With his jowled face and white hair he looks like a central-casting stereotype of a Southern senator. At age seventy-six, he has arrived at the zenith of his career, respected by conservatives and liberals alike as a man of unyielding principle and unassailable integrity and honesty.

Ervin views himself as a liberal in the Jeffersonian sense. Ironically, many of the "liberals" who excoriated him as a villain during the civil rights battles of the 1950s and the 1960s now heap praise on him as a protector of constitutional guarantees of liberty.

It is not so much Ervin who has changed as they. He has stood still and the world has turned. Some might argue that he has at times been inconsistent in his devotion to fundamental constitutional principles when the issue has been civil rights. But when one considers that Ervin still believes the significant threat to liberty lies in the tyranny of government and its insatiable thirst for power, his seeming inconsistencies tend to diminish to insignificance.

Ervin was born in Morganton, N.C., on September 27, 1896. He entered the University of North Caro-

lina at the age of sixteen. When America entered
World War I in 1917, he enlisted as a private in the
infantry, served in France, was wounded twice, and
was awarded the Silver Star for "conspicuous gal-
lantry" and the Distinguished Service Cross.

He was admitted to the North Carolina bar in
1919 and then, determined to acquire a better education and more legal training, entered Harvard Law
School as a third-year student. Even before he
earned his law degree in 1922, he was nominated
as the Democratic candidate for the North Carolina
legislature from Burke County. He ran and won.

Ervin practiced law and served three terms in the
state legislature. In 1935, he accepted an appointment as a county-court judge and another appointment in 1937 as a superior-court judge.

He served one term in Congress in 1946–47, but
did not seek reelection. In 1948, he was appointed to
the North Carolina Supreme Court, where he served
until 1954, when he was appointed to the United
States Senate following the death of Senator Clyde
Hoey.

Named to serve on the Senate committee to consider censure of Senator Joseph McCarthy for his
anticommunist witch-hunting excesses, Ervin played
a key role and proved his political courage.

Then Ervin helped carry the burden of Southern
resistance to school integration, open public accom-
modations, expansion of voting rights, and open
housing. Ervin always couched his arguments in
constitutional terms, arguing that the Supreme Court

had amended rather than interpreted the constitution.

More recently, Ervin has fought a wide range of constitutional battles, including determined opposition to expanded government wiretapping and surveillance, to no-knock and preventive-detention laws, and to the Equal Rights Amendment, which he contends would deprive women of many of the legal benefits they now enjoy. Nor did his Bible-belt constituency prevent him from fighting all attempts to amend the Constitution to permit prayer in public schools.

Seniority has given him powerful chairmanships, which he has used effectively to pass progressive legislation dealing with military justice, the rights of Indians, Federal bail reform, and limitations on the use of lie-detector tests.

Whether his actions draw the wrath of liberals or conservatives hardly seems to matter to Ervin as he follows his charted course. A thoughtful man who still seems to believe that the force of logic and the truth of arguments have a place in Senate debate, Ervin speaks in stately phrases that recall the golden age of oratory.

This book is an attempt to capture the flavor of Sam Ervin's ideas and language, as expressed in congressional debate and hearings. Every effort has been made to edit material so that it accurately reflects his meaning and avoids the error of the North Carolina preacher of seventy-five years ago.

As Chairman Sam relates the story: "At that time the women had a habit of wearing their hair in top-

Topknot Come Down!

knots. This preacher deplored that habit. As a consequence, he preached a ripsnorting sermon one Sunday on the text 'Topknot Come Down.' At the conclusion of his sermon, an irate woman, wearing a very pronounced topknot, told the preacher that no such text could be found in the Bible. The preacher thereupon opened the Scriptures to the seventeenth verse of the twenty-fourth chapter of Matthew and pointed to the words: 'Let him which is on the housetop not come down to take any thing out of his house.' "

If such contortions of context exist in the pages of this book, they are not intentional.

BILL M. WISE

Washington, D.C.
August, 1973

The Wisdom of Chairman Sam

WOMEN'S LIBERATION, SEX, AND MARRIAGE

Sam Ervin's attitude toward women and man-woman relationships is a combination of southern chivalry and traditional male chauvinism. He reveres motherhood, respects the institution of marriage, and appreciates the role of sex in the grand scheme of the universe. Thus, he is a leading opponent of Women's Lib and the Equal Rights Amendment.

This proposal [the Equal Rights Amendment] has been before the Congress for approximately the last fifty years, and up until approximately the last year or so, they couldn't find any people who were unintelligent enough to buy it.

ᐁ

If I may borrow the words of Omar Khayyam, I will say that the Equal Rights Amendment will undoubtedly shatter to bits what militant women deem

1

"this sorry scheme of things entire" but will not "re-mold it nearer to their heart's desire."

❧

Oh, how these militants who advocate equal rights for women must hate sex, to judge from their efforts in seeking to abolish it.

❧

The most important fact in life is sex.

❧

I am glad the Lord did create two sexes. I think it is one of the wisest things He has done. But, if He had had the benefit of some of the Women's Lib at the time of the creation, He would not have arranged things that way. We would have a unisex.

❧

The physiological and functional differences between men and women empower men to beget and women to bear children. From time whereof the memory of mankind runneth not to the contrary, custom and law have imposed upon men the primary responsibility for providing a habitation and a livelihood for their wives and children, to enable their wives to make the habitations homes, and to furnish nurture, care, and training to their children in their early years.

In this respect, custom and law reflect the wisdom embodied in the ancient Yiddish proverb that God could not be everywhere, so he created mothers. The physiological and functional differences between men

and women constitute life's most important reality.
Without them life could not exist. For this reason,
any country which ignores these differences when it
fashions its institutions and makes its laws is woe-
fully lacking in rationality.

෴

I came up in the horse-and-buggy days, when
farm couples used to ride to the market in a wagon
pulled by mules. Then, as now, there were a husband and a wife who did not always agree. They were
riding in a wagon to market and the two mules were
pulling in unison. You may not have come up in
those days, but they used to have a tongue that ran
between the mules to pull the wagon. The wife said
to the husband, "John, why in the world can't we
pull in double harness in the harmonious manner
that these two mules are doing?" And John said,
"Mary, you overlook the fact they only have one
tongue between them."

෴

I had a group [of Women's Libbers] come to my
office after I had spoken on the Senate floor against
[the Equal Rights Amendment]; some members of
their committee asked for an audience, which I
granted, and they asked me why I had spoken
against this amendment.

I pointed out that women would be drafted and
sent into combat, and these ladies, who were not
quite as ancient as I am, though some of them were
approximating that, said that that was exactly what

they wanted, that they wanted to be drafted and that they wanted to serve in combat.

I said, "Ladies, I have always tried to be a gallant gentleman. I have made a practice all of my life never to refer to a lady's age. But looking at you I am compelled to conclude that, despite your very youthful appearances, you are at least a month above the draft age. If you want to persuade me that women want to be drafted and sent out like the men to face the bullets of the enemy and to have their fair forms blasted into fragments by the enemy's bombs, you are going to have to send some of the sweet young things within the draft age up here to persuade me on that point."

∞

Sometimes I question the soundness of my conviction that women should not be converted into combat soldiers. If the militant women who demand that the Congress submit the Equal Rights Amendment to the states without changing a dot over an "i" or a cross over a "t" have the capacity to frighten the enemy like they frighten male politicians, the enemy might hoist the white flag without firing a shot.

∞

Some wise people even profess the belief that there may be psychological differences between men and women. To justify their belief, they assert that women possess an intuitive power to distinguish between wisdom and folly, good and evil.

∞

If you are going to abolish everything that has been abused, you would have to abolish sex, would you not?

∽

I think we can comprehend why some men are successful if we know their wives. When I was a student at the University of North Carolina I heard Horace Williams, professor of philosophy, speak to my class on the subject of the kind of girls we ought to marry.

He said we ought to marry a girl who would stand beside us as a tower of strength in good times and bad times, in joy and in sorrow, and in victory and defeat. He also said we should marry a girl who would make for us a good home in which we could find rest and relaxation, as well as inspiration.

∽

My life has been made happy by a wife who has stood beside me for many years and has faithfully performed all of the obligations devolving upon her as a wife and mother.

∽

To say these things is not to imply that either sex is superior to the other. It is simply to state the all-important truth that men and women complement each other in the relationships and undertakings on which the existence and development of the race depend.

POLITICS AND POLITICIANS

Sam Ervin has been active in politics for more than fifty years and, recognizing that government is a creature of politics, he perceives the politician's role as both worthy and necessary. But he also recognizes that politicians all too frequently fall victim to personal ambition and deceive both themselves and the people. Even as he defends the necessary role of politics, he does not hesitate to point out the follies of politicians.

Ostriches stick their heads in the sand to conceal reality from themselves. Politicians employ euphemistic words to hide reality from the people.

လ

That reminds me of a story. In some rural areas of North Carolina, those whose relatives are buried in small country churchyards gather annually and undertake to beautify them cooperatively by removing briars and weeds from graves and planting flowers beside them.

On one occasion the people had assembled in a certain churchyard to perform their yearly labor of love. One of them, who was somewhat lazy physically, hired George to accompany him and perform his physical tasks for him. George got down on his knees beside a grave and began to pull up the weeds. Suddenly he burst into laughter. His employer asked, "George, why are you laughing?" George replied, "It's them funny words that are writ on this gravestone," as he pointed to an epitaph which said "Not dead, but sleeping." George's employer said, "I don't see anything funny in that." George replied: "Boss, he ain't fooling nobody but himself."

The President and the sponsors of the revenue-sharing bill are not fooling anybody but themselves. The Federal government does not have a single diluted copper cent to share with anybody. On the contrary, all it has of a financial nature is a deficit which now amounts to $450 billion.

∞

The tragic fact is that the United States has had to borrow money to give away. If an individual were to borrow money for the purpose of giving it away, his family and his friends would institute an inquisition of lunacy and procure the appointment of a guardian to manage his affairs.

However, if an American politician advocates that the United States borrow money for the purpose of giving it away, he is likely to be elected President or chosen to be a member of the Senate or a member of the House of Representatives. And if he fails to attain any of these offices by the election route, he is most certain to be Secretary of State.

ᕲᕣᕲ

One clear thing about elections is that some men who are not willing to steal a penny of another man's money are willing to steal elections.

ᕲᕣᕲ

We cannot hope that everybody will be as honest as the two men who went to a cemetery in a county in my state to get names from the gravestones. One of them was reading the names off the gravestones, and the other was writing them down.

One man read: "Sacred to the memory of Israel Sherinstein."

The other man said: "Wait a minute. That's a long name. We can divide that into two parts and have two votes here."

The other fellow said: "No sir. If I'm going to have anything to do with this, it's going to have to be honest."

ᕲᕣᕲ

I would have been editor of the *Daily Tar Heel*, but I made a mistake. They had about sixteen of us in nomination for the post of editor of the *Tar Heel*, and in those days I was more modest than I am now. I wouldn't vote for myself in preference to somebody else. So I voted for a boy named Jimmy Hoover from High Point, and Jimmy beat me— Jimmy was elected with eight votes and beat me by one. So ever since then I have always voted for myself.

∞

Many years ago in Burke County two strong Democrats, Mark Berry and Uncle Jimmy Mull, lived on adjoining farms. A great argument arose over the location of the boundary line between the two farms. A lawsuit ensued. I don't know the outcome of the lawsuit, but they became so mad that they did not speak to each other for many years. After about ten years, Uncle Jimmy Mull was out plowing in the field and Mark Berry came over near the boundary line and said, "Good morning."

Uncle Jimmy said, "Mark Berry, what do you mean speaking to me after all these years of silence?"

Mark Berry said, "I just came over here to tell you that I'm going to run for sheriff on the Democratic ticket this fall, and I don't want you and your folks voting for me."

Uncle Jimmy told him, "Mark Berry, me and my folks have been voting on the Democratic ticket since Andy Jackson ran for President, and if you don't want me and my folks to vote for you, you will just have to keep your damn name off the Democratic ballot."

∞

Have you ever been a member of the great General Assembly of Virginia? I withdraw the question, because one time they called a character witness to the stand down in the North Carolina court

THE WISDOM OF SAM ERVIN 11

presided over by a good friend of mine, Judge Harlin
Johnston. The lawyer asked this witness, "Are you
a member of the state legislature?"

Judge Johnston said, "What are you trying to do,
impeach your own witness?"

Ⳝ

I know a lot of people who have been elected to
Congress from certain state legislatures and I don't
think they are a bit smarter since they came up here.

Ⳝ

Logic may say there is more wisdom in Washington than in the states, but I think experience shows
to the contrary.

Ⳝ

When I was a little boy I was elected to the North
Carolina Legislature, and my town philosopher Lum
Garrison came around, down to see me, and said,
"I want to give you some advice before you go down
as our legislator." He said, "Pass no more laws and
repeal half of those that we've already got." I think
that was pretty good advice, but I don't see any
prospects that the Congress is going to take it.

Ⳝ

Since I've been in the Congress, I've noticed that
a strange thing happens to many of us up here. We
stay too long in Washington, and we catch what is
commonly called "Potomac Fever." Potomac Fever
develops out of the purest of motives—that is, the
desire to do what we feel is best for our constituents

back home. In trying to assist our constituents, it seems that the feeling grows that the Federal bureaucracy can handle everything with much more wisdom than the people back home. We figure that those folks who were smart enough to send us up here have to be placed under the guardianship of a Federal bureaucracy.

∽

It is a very tragic truth of our age that many men in high position will no longer guard and defend liberty, but are ready to sacrifice it for votes.

∽

According to an old story, this event occurred in the British Parliament many years ago:

A member of the House of Commons introduced a bill which proposed that the British government should forthwith issue and sell enormous quantities of bonds, that the proceeds of the sale of the bonds should be immediately spent to finance existing temporary programs, and that no payment should be made on the principal of the bonds until fifty years had elapsed. Another member, whose economic views were similar to mine, denounced the bill on the ground that it was unfair to posterity. The author of the bill replied:

"Posterity has not done anything for me, and I'm not going to do anything for posterity. Besides, posterity can't vote in the next election." This old story ought to induce sorrow rather than merriment among us. This is so because it points up the fiscal

folly which has prevailed in the Federal government
for almost half a century.

∽

I happen to believe that Saint Paul spoke the
truth when he said in the eighth verse of the fifth
chapter of the first Epistle to Timothy: "But if any
provide not for his own, and specially for those of
his own house, he hath denied the faith and is worse
than an infidel."

Accordingly, when it comes to trying to promote
the prosperity of the textile industry and retain the
jobs for 323,000 North Carolinians who earn their
livelihood in that industry, I am going to stand on
Saint Paul and I think it is not only carrying out
good sound economy as far as the United States is
concerned, but involves a high standard of righteous
conduct.

∽

There is a story in the Bible, of course, about the
Pharisees who thanked God that they were not like
other men. There are too many politicians like that,
who stand up and say, "Thank God we are superior
to the southerners. Let us devote our attention to
improving them instead of engaging in any self-
improvement."

∽

I envy people who worry about sins far away from
home because it acts as an opiate and blinds them to
conditions existing on their own doorstep. It is a

whole lot easier to try to reform people far away from home than it is to reform your own constituents.

৩৵৩

I have been a southerner and perhaps not objective in appraising southerners. I am inclined to the opinion that if southerners had more influence in the government of this nation, we would have a better-ruled nation.

৩৵৩

I am sure all members of the Senate of my vintage received great pleasure at the time and some illumination from reading the cartoons concerned with the episodes in the fictitious lives of Maggie and her husband Jiggs. I recall one cartoon which showed that Maggie and Jiggs had taken a trip to Spain and Jiggs had found that there was a self-protection society of husbands over there called the Kazook Society.

Every member of the Kazook Society had taken a blood oath that he would come to the rescue of any other brother Kazook in the event that the brother Kazook was threatened or imperiled by his wife. So Jiggs immediately joined the Kazook Society.

He was walking down the streets of Madrid one day with Maggie, and Maggie sort of became dissatisfied with something Jiggs had done or said, and she immediately started to beat on Jiggs. So Jiggs gave the sign of distress to his brother Kazooks. He hollered, "Kazook." About a thousand Kazooks

came running to the rescue of Jiggs. Maggie took
an umbrella and laid them all out.

The last cartoon showed Jiggs in the hospital, all
swathed in bandages, and he was philosophizing:
"The idea behind the Kazook Society is pretty good,
but the trouble is it hasn't got enough members in it."

So the South never did have enough members in
the United States Senate to thwart the will of
seventy-eight Senators from other areas of this
country.

∽

It has been over one hundred years since General
Robert E. Lee surrendered at Appomattox. I am still
waiting for the day to arrive when a southern state
will be entitled to full recognition as a member of
this great United States.

∽

For approximately one hundred years nobody who
resides below the Mason-Dixon line has had a civil
right to aspire to the Presidency. Take Woodrow
Wilson. He wanted to be President. So he left the
place of his birth in Virginia and moved to New
Jersey. Grover Cleveland had a very far-seeing father
and mother. They wanted their son to be President.
So two years before Grover Cleveland was born
they moved from Virginia to the state of New York.

∽

I think government is a creature of politics and
I am for the freest and fullest discussion of both

government and politics. I don't think you can have
good government unless you have a lot of political
sparring.

ᔈ

A judge I know met a lawyer friend one day . . .
and the lawyer said, referring to some public question that was agitating the people of North Carolina
at the time, "I'd like to know what the people of
North Carolina think about this." So the judge said,
"When I want to know what the people think, I go
into my office, shut the door, sit down at my desk,
and communicate with myself." I would say about
the same thing goes for me.

ᔈ

Those in public life are sometimes subject to the
same experience as that of the young man who was
persuaded to become a candidate for the state legislature. His father tried to persuade him not to go
into politics. He said, "Son, don't go into politics.
If you get into this race for the legislature, before
it's over they will accuse you of stealing a horse."

The son did not take his father's advice. He
plunged into the race. After the election was over
he came back home, defeated. His father said, "Son,
didn't I say to you that you would be accused of
stealing a horse before the election was over?"

And the son replied, "Pa, it's much worse than
that. They durn near proved it on me."

ᔈ

The more vigilant you are, the more your representatives will voice your concern in Congress.

∾

All of us who hold public office get a certain amount of criticism. I get some myself. According to my friend, Francis Garrou, who operated a cotton mill in the town of Valdese in my home county, the criticism a public official receives proves he is qualified for his job.

On one occasion the election officials of the town of Valdese printed Francis Garrou's name on the town ballot as a candidate for mayor without his consent. This action irritated Francis to a high degree. He expressed his anger in a most emphatic manner to a cotton broker who called upon him to sell some cotton a few days before the election, stating that he would not qualify if he should be elected. Several weeks after the election the cotton broker made inquiry of Francis concerning the outcome of the Valdese town election.

Francis replied, "Those fools went ahead and elected me."

The cotton broker thereupon put this question to Francis: "Did you qualify as mayor?"

Francis replied, "I reckon I am qualified. I have been sworn in and cussed out, and if that does not qualify a man for public office in America, I don't know what does."

∾

I do not proscribe a man from public office who does not accept my sound views on all matters if he reaches what I consider to be honest conclusions different from mine.

ᗰᗷ

When I began practicing law in Morganton, North Carolina, the leading magistrate was William F. Hallyburton, otherwise known as Uncle Billy, who told me this story:

He had grown up on a farm. In the same neighborhood was a farm where "Carlton" Giles grew up. He and Carlton Giles ran together as boys—went swimming and fishing together. The families of both boys were Methodists. On one occasion they both went to a Methodist revival, and they were so moved by the preaching and singing that they got religion and joined the church together. They agreed to get down on their knees and pray for each other every day for as long as they lived.

As mature young men, they both became strong Democrats. In 1896, when the Populist movement was strong in North Carolina, Uncle Billy went to a Populist meeting. When he heard how the Populist party was going to be a panacea for correcting all the ills of the nation, he arose and avowed to join in the campaign.

At 2 A.M. the following morning, Uncle Billy was sound asleep when he was awakened by a loud knocking at his door. Uncle Billy asked, "Who is that knocking on my door at this hour of the night?"

Carlton Giles said, "Brother Billy, it is Carlton Giles."

Uncle Billy said, "Why are you knocking at my door at this ungodly hour?"

Carlton Giles replied, "I heard a foul slander on you as I was about to go to bed tonight. I immediately hitched up my horse and drove down here to hear you deny that slander with your own lips."

Uncle Billy said, "What foul slander did you hear, Carlton?"

Carlton Giles said, "I heard that you had left the Democrats and joined the Populists."

Uncle Billy said, "That is no slander; that is the truth."

Whereupon Carlton Giles said, "You remember when we were boys and we joined the church together and promised to get down on our knees and pray for each other every night for as long as we lived? Well, Brother Billy, I have kept that promise. Every night before I got into bed I have gotten down on my knees and in my supplication to the Almighty I have prayed for you. But, Brother Billy, from now on you can do your own goddamn praying!"

∞

I think elected officials of the government have the same freedom of speech as anyone else. After listening to an antiwar group for two hours and then hearing them tell me they were very offended by some speeches of Vice President Agnew, I told them that I also extended to Vice President Agnew the right of freedom of speech. I would like to point out that the Founding Fathers were not wise enough to devise any method in which freedom of speech was given to wise men only.

∞

Sometimes I think it would be a good thing if those in possession of power were to read documents which hold more wisdom regarding the crucial affairs of mankind than political platforms.

∞

I think from what I consider to be the financial state of my party that whatever you give you could charge off to charity.

∞

To be sure, the executive officials who deny the people their right to know what their government is doing always declare that they take such action in the public interest. Too often, however, one is compelled to suspect that such officials have confused the interest of the public with the interest of the Republican Party and withhold information for fear that it will disclose to the American people the folly of what they have done.

Unfortunately, bad habits, like measles, are contagious.

∞

I have been trying to reform Republicans all my life and have had virtually no success, but I would like for them to adopt good grammar and quit using the noun "Democrat" in lieu of the adjective "Democratic." If I can teach the Republicans that much grammar, I will feel that my effort to educate them has not been entirely in vain.

THE GOVERNMENT OF LAWS

As an attorney, a legislator, and a judge, Sam Ervin has devoted his life to the law. He has enormous respect for the law, but he does not believe all the problems which beset men can be solved by passing laws. Indeed, he thinks men deceive themselves when they become too dependent on laws and government and run the risk of exchanging liberty for governmental largesse.

It states in the Scriptures that Moses spent all day, all the time, judging cases, and his father-in-law told him, "You are breaking yourself down." He said, "Why don't you make a few laws for the guidance of other people and have somebody else down below you to judge all of the little cases?"

And that was the beginning of what we call the government of laws.

ᔈᔑ

21

And we have had the Ten Commandments for several thousand years and we still have violations of them.

෴

While authority to establish moral laws belongs to God, the authority to enact laws governing the conduct of men in an earthly society undoubtedly belongs to Caesar.

෴

Good government is government under a written constitution, which establishes a government of laws and puts it beyond the control of impatient public officials, temporary majorities, and the varying moods of public concern.

෴

By a government of laws, I mean a government in which certain and constant laws rather than the uncertain and inconstant wills of men govern all of the officers of government as well as the people at all times and under all circumstances.

෴

The men who composed the Constitutional Convention of 1787 comprehended in full measure the everlasting political truth that no man or set of men can be safely trusted with governmental power of an unlimited nature. In consequence, they were determined, above all things, to establish a government of laws and not of men.

෴

The duty of the citizen in a government of laws is obvious. It is to obey all laws without regard to whether he deems them just or unjust.

The duty of the lawyer in a government of laws is threefold in nature, regardless of whether he plays the part of the counselor or that of the advocate. He must know the law, be loyal to his client, and maintain his own integrity.

The judge is the cornerstone of the temple of justice. Upon him rests the most serious responsibility imposed upon any public officer in a government of laws. It is his duty to judge "his fellow travelers to the tomb" with absolute fairness according to the rules of law prescribed by the lawmakers of the state.

The American people have a simplistic faith in law. Our great national delusion is based on the fact that we have a childlike faith that anything wrong in our civilization can be abolished by law and that all of life's problems lend themselves to legal solutions. It is doubtful whether many people who are in custody in institutions for the mentally ill in our land suffer under a greater delusion than that.

We are an impatient people, who demand immediate solutions of our problems, no matter how difficult and enduring they may be. Besides, many of us are prone to ignore or rationalize unpleasant realities than to face them with forthrightness and fortitude.

ᘓ

No men of any race can legislate their way to the more abundant life. They must achieve such life by their own exertions and their own sacrifices. And anybody who maintains the contrary is either fooling himself or trying to fool somebody else.

If a man wants to drink cool water out of a spring on the top of a mountain, he ought to climb to the top of the mountain to get it. If he is unwilling to do that, he can, if he can bring enough pressure on government, induce government to pipe that water from the top of the mountain through governmental pipes, down to the valley where he is. But he will discover when he receives the water at the end of the governmental pipe that it has not only lost its coolness, but it has lost its taste, and become stale and flat, and is no longer desirable.

ᘓ

My observation is that whose bread I eat, his song I sing, and that is particularly true in the Federal government. I am against more Federal control, directly or indirectly.

ᘓ

Now, I have a small copy of the Constitution which covers 14 pages, and I want to invite your attention to the present laws we have on civil rights and regulations to enforce them. These present laws and regulations, instead of covering 14 pages, cover 1,213 pages, and this bill would add 73 additional pages.

Now, the regulations and laws we already have weigh 15 pounds 6 ounces. I would just like to know how many more pages and pounds, after Congress enacts this present bill into law, are we going to need before racial problems in America are solved in your judgment?

∞

It is the better part of wisdom to recognize that discriminations not created by law cannot be abolished by law. They must be abolished by changed attitudes in the society which imposes them.

∞

If we had some kind of miraculous power to amend people, it would work much better than amending the law.

∞

On one occasion when the Attorney General appeared before the Committee on the Judiciary and asked for increased powers in the voting-rights field, he was interrogated by me with respect to what he had done with the laws on the books. He said he had not used them; he just wanted more laws.

I told him he reminded me of a story they tell

down in my country about John and Mary who were courting each other, in the common parlance of North Carolina. One night they were sitting on a bench together in the moonlight with the fragrance of roses filling the air, and when the attending circumstances were such as to inspire romantic feelings, John said to Mary, "Mary, if you wasn't what you is, what would you like to be?"

Mary said, "John, if I wasn't what I is, I would like to be an American Beauty rose."

Then Mary turned the question on John and said, "John, if you wasn't what you is, what would you like to be?"

And John said, "Mary, if I wasn't what I is, I would like to be an octopus."

Mary said, "What is an octopus?"

John said, "An octopus is some kind of a fish or something that has a thousand arms."

And Mary said, "John, if you was an octopus and had a thousand arms, what would you do with all those arms?"

John said, "Mary, I would put every one around you."

Mary said, "Go away, John. You ain't used the two you already got."

So we have all those attorneys in the Justice Department. They will not use all of the laws they already have, and they come down here asking for more laws and more laws, until the books are cluttered with laws on voting rights.

Why any human being thinks if you had two laws instead of one you could get them enforced any better, I can't imagine.

∽

Ironically, the Free Society has become the most law-ridden society in the history of the world.

∽

If anything is wrong you say, "Pass a law." We don't stop to inquire how many laws are already on the books on that subject, and whether they're efficacious.

∽

I think you would agree with me in the observation that the experience of the human race indicates it is very hard to make any kind of a law or any kind of a regulation which will be both knaveproof and foolproof.

∽

I test the wisdom of the law not upon what a good man can do with it, but what a bad man can do with it. . . .

Apart from constitutional considerations, no-knock laws are bad. If its people are to have respect for law, a nation must have respectable laws, and no law is respectable if it authorizes officers to act like burglars, and robs the people of the only means they have for determining whether those who

seek to invade the habitations violently or by stealth
are officers or burglars.

ɔ~ɔ

Good government may be thwarted to a sub-
stantial degree by venal men. Fortunately, however, the number of such men in public office is
comparatively small, and the injury they do to good
government is not wholly without remedy.

It is otherwise with respect to public men whose
good intentions prompt them to govern by their own
notions of what they deem to be desirable rather
than by the rules established by our government
of laws. They not only thwart good government,
but they also jeopardize the existence of our government of laws itself.

ɔ~ɔ

No one man and no one executive department
should have the absolute power to order government spying on how people use their right of free
speech. This is what we mean by a government of
laws and not of men.

ɔ~ɔ

Ours is not a country in which government can
become a tyranny against the will of the people. But
tyranny can come just as surely if the people are
willing to deliver over their freedom in search for
safety. It is incumbent on every citizen to resist the
temptation to excuse constitutional excesses in the
name of "law and order."

BUREAUCRATS AND THE BUREAUCRACY

Although he understands and appreciates the contribution which dedicated public employees make to our society and the vital role they play, Sam Ervin approaches the Federal bureaucracy with the healthy skepticism of the North Carolina hill country. He is always prepared with a pointed comment to prick the bureaucratic balloons of those who fly too high.

A good many years ago I bought a book which has a little poem which is translated from the Chinese [and is] supposed to be written about 2,500 or 3,000 years ago. In this poem, this prosperous Chinese farmer, who was anticipating the early birth of a son, expressed the hope that his son would not be too bright or too energetic. He says, in this poem, if his son is not too bright or too energetic that he might well enter government service and enjoy a very special and uneventful life. If he

29

didn't exercise too much intelligence or energy, he might wind up as a cabinet minister or something.

∽

I have long entertained the idea that maybe people in government service are like people outside of government service. We have some people that you might call leaders, and others followers, and some who you might call pussyfooters.

Now, if a man wants to lead a peaceful and un-eventful and tranquil life in government service or in life itself, he can refrain from making decisions, especially in controversial matters, and do just as little beyond drawing his breath and his salary as possible, and in that way he is not likely to stir up any great antagonism.

Then there is another group, not only in life but in government service, that you might call followers, who are very dedicated people, who try to learn what their duties are according to orders and regulations prescribed by those in authority and who try to carry out those duties. They are the people that really probably number most of us, and keep the world functioning.

Then there is a third group of people who are the people that I call leaders, who make decisions. They have to make decisions in light of the facts known to them at the time that they make their decisions. Unlike those who later condemn them for wrong decisions, they don't have the benefit of hindsight in advance.

∽

One of the great problems in delegating authority
to unelected bureaucrats is the fact that if you give
them an inch of authority they immediately steal a
mile.

∽   *aesop*

SENATOR JOHNSTON: Your objection, then, is that
we are delegating not only to the President, but
maybe any little head of any department, a right to
legislate which the Constitution gives only to the
Congress of the United States?

SENATOR ERVIN: The Senator is correct. The
Senator is familiar with the old fable of Aesop about
the lion in which he invited another animal into his
den to pay him a visit. The animal said, "I am not
coming. I notice that all of the tracks of those who
have accepted your invitations in times past lead
into your den and none of them come out." The
Federal government never surrenders power once
given it.

∽

I have nothing in particular against Federal
bureaucrats except I don't want to be ruled by any
of them.

∽

As a lawyer who has watched these administrative
agencies work, I fear them because there is a tendency, especially in those which deal with emotional
problems, such as controversies between management and labor, for such problems to be controlled

by crusaders who are devoted to a cause rather than the administration of justice.

∽

Worse than ironic, on some subjects those who write these administrative rules and regulations—which have the effect of law in every sense—have so twisted and distorted the parent statutes that Congress seems to perform a useless exercise by enacting a law.

∽

Andrew Johnson made a statement that I think all Americans ought to read and memorize. He said, speaking of government officials:

"Outside of the Constitution, we have no powers save those that all citizens have, and within the Constitution we have no powers except those which the Constitution gives us."

∽

If we take what the political doctors say about smoking cigarettes and what the other doctors say about sugar, we are likely to come to the conclusion that we ought to do what is outlined in this little verse:

Cholesterol is poisonous,
    so never, never eat it.
Sugar, too, may murder you,
    there's no way to beat it.
Some foods were filled with vitamins
    till processing destroyed it.
So let your life be ordered
    by each documented fact,

And die of malnutrition
   with your arteries intact.

And warily watch every sunny sky for bolts of
lightning.

cx

I am still going to fight for the liberty of the
citizens of the United States to make foolish decisions by themselves rather than having wise
decisions made for them by the most benevolent
bureaucrat.

cx

I will have to say in light of the fact that the
Department [of Agriculture] canceled 1961 allotments, refused to issue 1962 allotments, and
assessed a penalty of over a half million dollars
against Billie Sol Estes, that it reminds me of the
kind of favoritism or favors that Irvin S. Cobb gave
to an old friend.

Cobb said many years ago that after he had left
Kentucky and moved to New York he paid a visit
back to his home town in Kentucky. In the course
of this visit he saw an immense crowd of people
gathered together. His curiosity was aroused and he
went to where the crowd was gathered. He saw there
was a scaffold erected to hang somebody. He looked
up on the scaffold and found one of his old boyhood
chums that he had gone fishing with. And another
one of his old boyhood chums was deputy sheriff
who was apparently there for the purpose of officiat-
ing at the hanging of his other old chum.

He said when he got close to the platform, the deputy sheriff called him up there and said, "You know, under the law of Kentucky, this man who has been sentenced to death can't be hanged unless the death warrant is read to him. Unfortunately, the sheriff is gone and he has deputized me to do the hanging, and I can't read and I wondered if you would mind coming up on the platform and reading the death warrant to the condemned."

Irvin Cobb said he went up on the platform pursuant to the request of the deputy sheriff. He read the death warrant to his old chum. When he got through reading the death warrant and having thus made it possible to have his old chum hang him according to the law of Kentucky, his old chum said to him: "Thank you, Irvin, thank you. I knew that if there was ever a favor you could do for me, you would sure do it."

∞

It is sometimes hard to find rhyme or reason to some actions of government officials. This is because, in Washington, the fashions in follies change not only year by year, but sometimes day by day.

∞

I think one of the unfortunate things about big government is that it does move very slowly. That is one reason I ordinarily vote to keep as much government as close to home as possible.

∞

I personally hate to see everybody coming to the Federal government to get money which the Federal government does not have to solve their problems. I think it presages the destruction of our federal system of government.

ᐧᐧᐧ

Manifestly, the political subdivisions of the country, such as states, municipalities, and counties, can know much better than the national Congress, sitting in Washington, what the problems of the various communities are and what is the best way to solve those problems. That was the genius of the Constitution. The Founding Fathers provided that as much government should be kept near the people as was possible. They realized something which the American people are again coming to realize slowly, but are about to realize painfully and speedily: that when you concentrate all the powers of government in the Federal government, you are going to find such concentration of powers incompatible with the continuance of the liberties of the people.

ᐧᐧᐧ

I have heard a great deal said by public men about Federal-state partnerships, but I have noticed that in carrying out the partnership that the Federal government affords about 99.9 per cent of the direction of the affairs of the partnership, and the state carries out its partnership by obeying the directions of the Federal government.

ᐧᐧᐧ

It is said we must continue the Civil Rights Commission as a valued symbol of the civil-rights movement. Even without this commission, however, we have more civil-rights bureaucracies skittering across the face of the Federal government than Congress can keep track of. Before long we will have more monuments to civil rights than we have rights.

∽

It [the Subversive Activities Control Board] has already been gratuitously extended four times: twice for two years, then for one year, and last time for four years. Now we have been asked to grant it life for an additional five years to complete work that we were originally assured could be done in two years.

∽

Not only is this supposedly transitory body still with us, but, like all bureaucracies, it has grown in size and costs in inverse proportion to the value of the work it has produced.

∽

There is nothing under the sun more permanent than a temporary Federal agency. The U.S. Spruce Production Corporation was established during the last eighty-four days of World War I as a temporary emergency measure for the production and allocation of aircraft lumber. It was still in existence in December, 1946.

∽

acronym

I doubt seriously whether any member of Congress could tell us how many Federal agencies we have.

∾ *U. S. 9 A*

SENATOR ERVIN: Pardon me, I do not understand what U.S. of A. means.

WITNESS: That is Under Secretary of the Army, Mr. Chairman. We have all sort of acronyms.

SENATOR ERVIN: Sounds like United States of America to me. I have difficulty remembering all these abbreviations. U.S. of A. is United States of America.

WITNESS: Well, you are not alone. Even after two years I have great difficulty, but the reason I thought we had to leave it here is that we are quoting from a document. But I am with you. They confuse me, too.

∾

When I start to reading Federal regulations, I find several cases of incurable mental indigestion in each sentence.

∾ *Caligula*

In ancient days in Rome there was an emperor named Caligula, and Caligula wrote his laws in small letters and hung them up so high on the walls that people could not read them and know what the laws were.

But as compared with the practices of the Office of Federal Contract Compliance, Caligula was a most enlightened legislator and administrator, because if a person got a ladder long enough and a magnifying glass big enough, he could have climbed up and read Caligula's laws. But one cannot read the constantly changing minds of the officials of the Office of Contract Compliance in the Department of Labor.

∽

The fact is there is no uniformity among the different departments [of government]. Some years ago, I requested a specific report on American imports from Japan from the State Department as well as the Department of Commerce. Both gave me a copy of the report. The copy from the Department of Commerce was not classified in any respect, while the Department of State copy was classified and it was turned over to me on the condition that I wouldn't make any part of it public, under any circumstances.

∽

I have been here as a member of this committee for many days, and watched the efforts of the Department of Commerce and the Department of State to withhold from the Congress and the American people information about the matter we are investigating. It all reminds me of the story that Governor Bob Taylor, of Tennessee, used to tell about the farmer who drove his team of mules to market one day with a load of cabbage, and took his idiotic son along with him to hold the mules. When he got to town, he had to go off on a matter of business, and left the son to hold the mules. He said, "Son, don't say anything to anybody, because if you do they will find out you are a fool."

The farmer went off and a merchant came up and asked the boy, "Son, what do you want for your cabbage?"

The boy, remembering his father's injunction, being under orders of secrecy, made no effort to reply. The merchant asked him two or three times, "What do you want for your cabbage?" And being bound by the secrecy injunction of his father, the son said nothing. And the merchant said, "You are a fool," and turned around and walked off.

By that time, the father came back, and the son hollered out, "Hey, Pop, they found it out and I never said a word."

∽

When I was a student at Chapel Hill, I sat at the feet of a much beloved professor of geology, Collier Cobb. I remember little of what he taught about the history and structure of the earth, but I recall verbatim this pungent witticism of his:

"Wise men learn from the experience of others; fools learn from their own experience; but most of us learn neither from the experience of others nor from our own."

Measured by this standard, the financial policy-makers of the Federal government do not possess the wisdom of fools.

∽

I have to confess I was astounded when I first saw one of those forms on the 1967 economic census as it applied to law firms. I am still curious to know what interest the government has in collecting information of this character and what it is going to do with it after it gets it. In other words, I am reminded on this last point of an old story they tell about the little dog that ran after the express train barking. Somebody standing by said, "What is the dog going to do with it if he catches it?"

I was astounded yesterday that one of the questions contained in questionnaires to retired military persons was "Are you right-handed or left-handed?"

I could see how a manager of a ball club, looking for a pitcher, would ask a man if he is right-handed or left-handed, but what business is it of the government asking retired military personnel, who have already served their government, whether they are right- or left-handed? To put it in plain English, that is a damnfool question.

I have some of these forms. [To] keep them from getting mixed up, they have put different colors on them. Some are green, some brown, and some are blue. I would venture to suggest that an awful lot of small businessmen are rather blue when they receive one of them.

They tell us when we leave this world we take nothing with us, but I expect I will take my Social Security card. I am just afraid if I got to the Pearly

Gates—if I get that far toward Paradise—Saint Peter might not let me in unless I can show my number.

လ

I might add, the reason I am somewhat disturbed by the indiscriminate use of Social Security numbers for all purposes is the fact that when the government reduces all of us to the status of a number, that number is going to be zero.

IN DEFENSE OF THE CONSTITUTION

Sam Ervin believes the genius of the Constitution is that it struck a workable balance between the need for government and the rights of free men. But he knows it is a delicate balance, needing constant attention lest it topple toward tyranny on the one side or anarchy on the other. As a reminder, he carries with him a copy of the Constitution and is quick to quote from it whenever he feels Supreme Court Justices, Presidents, or his fellow Senators are forgetting or ignoring its principles.

The Founding Fathers . . . understood that a nation which disregards the lessons of history is doomed to repeat the mistakes of the past. They desired to spare the nation they were creating this tragic experience.

These things inspired the Founding Fathers to dream Earth's most magnificent dream.

They dreamed they could enshrine a government of laws conforming to the eternal truths taught by

43

history in a written Constitution, and make that
government operate in accordance with their intent
by entrusting the interpretation of that Constitution to a Supreme Court composed of fallible men.

To this end, they framed the Constitution, which
they intended to last for the ages and to constitute
"a law for rulers and people" alike at all times and
under all circumstances.

ᴄᴠᴏ

It is manifest that the Constitution cannot operate
as the supreme law of the land unless its meaning is
fixed, that is, established, and unless its meaning is
unchanging, that is, stable.

ᴄᴠᴏ

The Constitution was written to put restraints on
government. The Founders rejected the theory that
the liberty of a free people should depend on the
self-restraint of the governors.

ᴄᴠᴏ

Unfortunately, constitutions are not self-executing
and cannot save freedom unless love for freedom
abides in the hearts of the people.

ᴄᴠᴏ

I do not believe that either our country or any
human being within our borders has any security
against tyranny on the one hand or anarchy on the
other unless Presidents and Congresses and Supreme
Court Justices are faithful to the precepts of the
Constitution.

ᴄᴠᴏ

As you know, we hear frequent charges nowadays that the form of government provided by the Constitution is inappropriate to the needs of modern times. All of the three basic concepts embodied in that document—constitutionalism, federalism, and separation of powers—are thought by many to be outmoded means of carrying on affairs in the twentieth century when all governments must be "crisis governments" in order to survive. I, for one, emphatically do not believe that. I believe the deficiencies in our governmental structure result, not from adherence to the notion of federalism and separation of power, but rather from departure from them.

∽

I know that in recurring to fundamental principles I lay myself open to the charge that I am setting the clock back. As one who believes truth to be eternal, I am not troubled by this charge. Moreover, I have observed that the charge is usually made by those who labor under the delusion that there was little, if any, wisdom on earth before they arrived. It was a wise man and not a wag who suggested that these persons object to setting the clock back because it would require them to adjust their clocks and their minds forward.

∽

There is an old story that illustrates the reluctance which characterizes all of us in certain areas. A gentleman, who was rather prominent in his community, attained his ninety-fifth birthday anniversary. On that day the newspaper reporters came around to interview him. And one of them asked how old he was. He said, "This is my ninety-fifth birthday anniversary."

And the reporter said, "Well, you have lived a long, long time and have seen many changes in your life."

And he said, "Yes, and I was against every one of them."

∾

When I get to thinking about the disrepute into which our Constitution has fallen, I am reminded of the tragedy of one whom I shall call Jim.

Jim had the misfortune to be run over and killed by a train. His administrator brought suit against the railroad for damages for wrongful death. In order to prove that Jim had actually been run over and killed by a train, the administrator called as a witness a man who testified that immediately before the tragedy he saw Jim walking up the railroad track. Then he saw the train come up. He said that the train passed between him and Jim and that after the train had passed he could not see Jim anywhere.

The witness then testified that he walked up the track in the direction in which he had seen Jim walking and that as he got some little distance up the track, he looked over and he saw Jim's left arm, dismembered from his body, lying on the right side of the track. He said that he walked a little farther, looked on the left side of the track, and saw Jim's head and a part of his chest. As he walked up the track, he saw the remainder of Jim's body.

Then the lawyer asked the witness, "When you saw these gruesome relics, what did you do?"

The witness replied, "I said to myself, 'Something serious must have happened to Jim.' "

Well, something serious has happened to the Constitution.

∽

Some years ago the late distinguished Senator from Illinois, Mr. Dirksen, had a resolution pending in the Judiciary Committee to set aside a certain week in September as Constitution Week. He was seated on the opposite side of the table from me, and made this inquiry of me before the Committee began its deliberations:

"I trust that you will support my resolution to set aside a certain week in September as Constitution Week."

I said, "I certainly will. I have always believed we ought to pay homage and tribute to our beloved dead."

∽

I am always intrigued by this question of the Constitution as a living document. I think it is a living document, but that the term is often used by men to justify their theory that the Supreme Court should disregard the Constitution and go and substitute their personal notions for constitutional principles. If that is what the Constitution is, then the Constitution is not a living document. It is a dead document and the judges as executors can dispose of its remains any way they see fit.

∽

I believe the Supreme Court committed "verbicide" upon the words of the Constitution when they handed those decisions down. I borrowed the term "verbicide" from Oliver Wendell Holmes. He believed life and language were alike sacred. The violent treatment of a word which destroys its legitimate meaning, its life, is forbidden just as homicide is forbidden.

∽

I believe also that those of us who love and revere the Constitution must continue to discharge our duty to carefully scrutinize the decisions of the Court and to comment fearlessly upon those decisions that we believe to endanger the continued existence of constitutional government in America.

∽

In the final analysis, those who contend that Supreme Court Justices are justified in changing the meaning of constitutional provisions while pretending to interpret them confuse right and power.

∽

After all, the rulings of Supreme Court Justices are not sacrosanct. Indeed, they are entitled to respect only if they are respectable, and they are not respectable if they do violence to the language of the Constitution.

∽

I think the Constitution intends a Justice to be independent. But I do not think it contemplates he is going to be independent of the Constitution.

∽

Our duty . . . is to determine how to protect the rights of all Americans of all races and all generations without extinguishing other precious rights. Our duty is to implement the Constitution without perverting it.

∽

Those who seek to rob southern states and their officials and people of basic government and legal rights by civil-rights legislation incompatible with the Constitution established for all Americans have a fifth column in the South. The fifth column consists of southern whites who wrong Negroes. These southern whites commit a twofold wrong. First, they wrong the Negroes who are their victims; and, second, they lend aid and comfort to those who strive to defeat us in our fight to preserve America's birthright for all Americans of all generations and all races.

∽

I have been generally reluctant to advocate alterations to the Constitution of the United States. History has proven it to be one of the most wisely drafted documents of all time. The framework of government it establishes and the protection of individual liberty it incorporates have served our people well.

∽

And when the Constitution of the United States is nullified by those in authority because of their impatience or because of their zeal to do what they consider to be advisable, liberty in America has no chance to survive; because then we will have a government of men and not a government of laws.

∽

I think we are in a serious condition when so many men are willing to destroy fundamentals for the sake of accomplishing, in a hurry, objectives that they deem to be desirable.

∽

The Supreme Court has the power to interpret the Constitution. The power to amend the Constitution belongs to the states and to Congress. There is a great difference between the power to amend the Constitution and the power to interpret it. That difference is as wide as the great gulf which yawned between Lazarus in Abraham's bosom and Dives in Hell.

The power to interpret the Constitution is the power to state its meaning. The power to amend it is the power to change its meaning. The Supreme Court of the United States does not have the power to change the meaning of the Constitution.

∽

I venture to suggest that any Supreme Court Justice who prefers to amend the Constitution and make laws rather than interpret them ought to lay aside his judicial robes, enter the political arena by seeking election to the Senate or House of Representatives, and thus give the people, from whom all the just powers of government are derived, an opportunity to declare by their votes whether they approve or disapprove his proposals for remaking our governmental and legal institutions and our society in his own image.

∽

You know, those of us who do not fully approve of the action of the Supreme Court during recent years are sometimes criticized by those who say we are making attacks on the Court. I get no pleasure out of saying the things I have. But I took an oath as a Senator and as a voter to support the Constitution of the United States, and I have to perform some unpleasant things in connection with the performance of this oath.

∽

It is not easy for me to express my disapproval of Supreme Court action. I was taught in my youth by my father, a practitioner at the North Carolina bar for sixty-five years, to revere the Supreme Court as the guardian of the Constitution. When I was a small boy, he took me to the Supreme Court chamber, pointed out the busts of great jurists of the past, and said with reverential awe:

"The Supreme Court will abide by the Constitution, though the heavens may fall."

I regret to say, however, that the course of the Supreme Court in recent years has been such as to cause me to ponder the question whether fidelity to fact ought not to induce its members to remove from the portal of the building which houses it the majestic words, "Equal Justice Under the Law," and to substitute for it the inscription, "Not Justice Under Law, But Justice According to the Personal Notions of the Temporary Occupants of this Building."

∽

To my mind, the office of Chief Justice of the United States is probably of greater importance than that of President of the United States. If you get a President, and you do not like his official acts, you have a way to rid yourself of him in four years. If you get a Justice of the Supreme Court and find that he does not manifest as much devotion to the Constitution as he does to his personal notions, the country has to put up with him for his lifetime.

∽

Now let me make it very plain I am not saying any of the Justices of the Supreme Court are bad men; but candor does compel me to confess that I think that any judge, whether he is on the Supreme Court or any other court, who is unable or unwilling to subject himself to the restraint which is inherent in the judicial process, when that process is understood and applied, is imprudent.

Now, the restraint which is inherent in the judicial process is simply the ability and the willingness of an occupant of judicial office to lay aside his personal notions of what a law or a constitutional principle ought to have said, and be guided solely by what the law or constitutional principle does say. And I say this in all seriousness, as one who has studied the decisions of the Supreme Court with as much diligence as time and other duties permit—that I greatly fear the road to destruction of constitutional government in America is being paved with great rapidity by the good intentions of Supreme Court Justices.

∞

When I refer to a court as "activist" I mean a court which ignores the history or policy or settled precedents behind a particular clause of the Constitution or statute which it is interpreting. The Supreme Court can be labeled "activist" whether it is popularly considered "liberal" as was the Warren court, or as conservative. And whether as a liberal activist court or as a conservative activist court, the vice is the same. An activist court puts its own views on what the Justices believe the Constitution should say above what the Constitution in fact does say.

∞

We used to have a retired naval chaplain in my home town named Edmundson. He was a Methodist preacher and a very fine preacher, before he became a naval chaplain. And then he went into the Navy, and he made a fine sailor. He not only made a fine sailor, but he learned to cuss, like sailors are reputed to cuss. And so he retired and came back to my town, which was his home town, and sometimes he lapsed into the habits of a sailor, and he cussed. And so some of the people that did not approve of a preacher cursing, they went to the local Methodist

preacher and asked him to remonstrate with Brother
Edmundson about his evil ways. So this man saw
Brother Edmundson and told him it was reported
to him that he cursed and he said, "I have even
heard on occasion you go so far as to take the Lord's
name in vain."

And Chaplain Edmundson said, "Brother, it is
true I do curse, and it is true that sometimes I take
the Lord's name in vain, but, brother, I would have
you understand that I always do so with the utmost
reverence."

Everything I have said about decisions of the
courts and nominees has been said with the utmost
reverence for the Court as an institution.

∽

During prohibition days, my father used to say
that John Barleycorn had more enemies in public
and more friends in private than any gentleman of
his acquaintance. I wish I could put the Constitution
of the United States on a plane with John Barleycorn today. I would say that, judging by the proposal to extend the Voting Rights Act of 1965, the
Constitution of the United States has an abundance
of enemies in public and very, very few friends
either in public or in private.

∽

It is high time government officials stopped talking
so much about management concepts and returned
to constitutional concepts.

∽

To help in the business of governing and managing, they have pressed into service the wonders of our scientific age in the form of computers, microfilm, laser beams, sophisticated photographic and electronic recording equipment, and many new techniques for rapid electronic communications. These amazing machines and devices not only expand the memory of a man a trillionfold, they extend enormously his ability to retrieve instantly the information stored, integrate it with other information, and send it across-country or around the world.

I have some examples here of the progress in this area. This book is the Bible as we have always known it. This particular family Bible weighs eleven pounds. Contrast it with this piece of microfilm, two by two inches, which contains on it 1,245 pages of a Bible, with all the 773,746 words of it. This means a reduction of 62,500 to one. With such a process, I am told all the millions of books stored on the 270 miles of shelves in the Library of Congress could be reproduced on slides and be stored in six filing cabinets. They can be retrieved and read with a simple student microscope or magnifying device.

Someone remarked that this meant the Constitution could be reduced to the size of a pinhead. I said I thought maybe that was what they had done with it in the executive branch because some of those officials could not see it with their naked eyes.

∞

Our system of government, with its powers separated between three coordinate branches, is not the most efficient ever devised, nor was it ever meant to be.

∾

If those who possess the power to rekindle the dream of the Founding Fathers and to preserve the right of the people to constitutional government do not act, Americans will learn with agonizing sorrow the tragic truth taught by Justice Sutherland:

"The saddest epitaph which can be carved in memory of a vanished liberty is that it was lost because its possessors failed to stretch forth a saving hand while yet there was time."

∾

I have attempted unsuccessfully to persuade the Senate to adopt various amendments to this bill. My motive for doing so has been as lofty as the motive which actuated the conduct of Job Hicks in my county at the turn of the century. At that time there was in the county a skilled bricklayer named John Watts. John felt called to preach, and while he was very proficient in the art of bricklaying, he was somewhat deficient in theology.

Nonetheless, John persuaded some of the local churches to let him use their pulpits on Sunday. On one particular Sunday, Job Hicks happened by. Job had had several drinks of Burke County corn liquor, which is alleged to be a very potent beverage. When he heard John exhorting the congregation, Job staggered up the aisle, grabbed John Watts by the coat collar, and threw him out of the church.

Job Hicks was prosecuted for disturbing religious

worship, but the judge, feeling like Job Hicks that there might be some deficiencies in the theological doctrines being expounded by John Watts at the time of the unseemly event, suggested that Job must have been too intoxicated to realize what he was doing. Job Hicks responded, "Your Honor, it is true that I had had several drinks of corn liquor, but I would not want your Honor to think that I was so drunk that I could stand by and see the word of the Lord mummicked up without doing something about it."

So, I have offered amendments to this bill because I did not wish to see the Constitution of the United States mummicked up.

THE AGE OF TECHNOLOGY

Sam Ervin recognizes the necessity of employing modern computer technology to increase governmental efficiency and enable it to deal with the increasingly complex problems of an increasingly complex age. But he believes the computer is not endowed with the qualities of infallibility, compassion, and forgiveness and therefore should not be allowed to play God with the lives of American citizens.

We live in a world increasingly controlled by experts and technicians. Men who should know better are afraid to speak up when they see other government officials violating or proposing violation of individual rights in pursuit of some goal. They fear the power of the specialist or the efficiency expert who claims the necessity of some method or policy in order to make a rational decision. The result is that we are becoming overly awed by scientific claims to validity and efficiency. The result is that we stand in danger of letting technology—the creed of efficiency, the dogma of the expert—become the religion of our culture.

We live in the dawn of a day which may well see rationality in decision-making elevated to the status of a religious dogma which will dominate the minds of man. And I submit that its tyranny, if unchecked, will take a toll unequaled by that of any form of political tyranny in man's history.

If this seems a bleak outlook, I do not think it an exaggerated one. The more I hear and read and witness of haphazard plans for computerized data systems, of the goal-oriented practices perpetuated by government or great corporations on employees and other citizens, the more I believe we are losing track of certain fundamental truths by which we once piloted our national course.

We are forgetting, I believe, that in the diversity of our religious faiths and denominations, we have cherished one national religion—that is, humanity and the dignity of the individual. This idea has been the amulet of our form of government and of the society in which we live. When we have tolerated departure from it, even by a few, it has been to our national sorrow.

⁓

I used to say that I heard so many marvelous things about computers that I was going to introduce an amendment to the Presidential election system to make a computer eligible for election to the Presidency. Then I studied it a little bit and I was told a computer could make a logical deduction from the facts stored in its memory bank but could not make an illogical deduction from the data. I withdrew my amendment because anything that cannot make an illogical deduction from the data is not qualified to be a politician.

ᕮᐧᕭ

Now, I used to practice law and I found that rural jurors in the area in which I live have a superstitious awe about bloodhounds and any testimony of bloodhounds tracking a suspect. And I find almost the same kind of superstitious awe about the computer.

ᕮᐧᕭ

We all have a superstitious awe, I think, about the computer and its ability to store and retrieve information, and to analyze information. We have to recognize that most of the dangers which the computer poses arise out of human beings rather than technology.

ᕮᐧᕭ

One of the most alarming trends I have noticed where electronic data-processing is used on a large scale is an attempt to transfer responsibility to the computer for mistakes in executive judgment or faulty evaluation of the data. This is obviously the most important single factor to be considered in the entire computer movement. For a machine has no ethics or morality.

ᕮᐧᕭ

The wonders and the threats of the New Technology point up the need, then, for a special type of education—a spiritual education.

The need of civilized men for communicating the legacies of the race is an axiom wherever educators meet; but in our society, under the Constitution, for the age of technology in which we dwell, it is even more essential that we communicate the spiritual legacies of our history as a Republic. Only then will citizens be properly equipped to judge the morality of those who govern.

ᴄᴠᴐ

Next, I would try to spread a gospel of my own. That is my belief that while the Recording Angel drops a tear occasionally to wash out the record of our human iniquities, there is no compassion to be found in computers. Nor is it to be found in all the new instruments for measuring man which the behavioral sciences and the New Technology hold out to us.

ᴄᴠᴐ

In other words, a computer has a most remarkable memory, never forgets anything, but it has no heart and it has no forgiveness.

ᴄᴠᴐ

Once a vast information-gathering and processing program is put to work, it will take years to undo the harm done or to trace the flow of data on an individual in order to destroy files and microfilm.

ᴄᴠᴐ

We want to enjoy the benefits of the efficiency which computers afford to government and to business and to learning, but at the same time we want to make as certain as is humanly possible that the privacy of individuals will not be destroyed on the altar of efficiency.

⚭

It is the computer which contains information about the individual which discloses what his thoughts are, what his activities are, his physical and psychological conditions, things of that kind that pose the threat to privacy.

⚭

The computer field is so vast that talking about it is like the story of the two elderly ladies in a town in North Carolina. They entertained the new young preacher on Sunday afternoon, and then invited him to dinner that evening. He said he had to preach at Sunday evening service first, so one of the ladies stayed home to prepare dinner and the other went with the preacher to the church. When they returned after the services, the one who had stayed home asked how he had preached. The other lady said he had preached in the apostolic style. He just took the gospel and preached all over the place.

⚭

Our officials have learned that the easier it becomes to use computers to obtain and store information of all kinds about people, the easier it becomes to substitute surveys and "people-studies" for judg-

ment and creative ingenuity in the administration
of the laws.

❧

One of the great psychological harms resulting
from the computerizing of a private nature about
people, about their thoughts and their political
activities, is that people will try to conform to what
they think the image of the majority should be.

❧

I once jokingly mentioned that the day may come
when we will replace politicians with computers.
Judging from some of the reasoning of politicians
I've seen over the years, I know I would sooner take
the logic of a computer. The machine may suffer the
same lack of intelligence as some politicians, but
at least there is consistency in its idiocy.

❧

There is an increasing belief that anything scientific must be more reliable and rational than the
judgment of men. Unfortunately, this is true not
only of officials who favor the lie-detector machine;
it is also true of the average person who is subjected
to it. Officials have admitted that its greatest use is
in scaring the individual into admitting his trans-
gressions.

There is a growing belief that the machine can
bridge that credibility gap which must exist wherever
fallible men choose between truth and untruth.

But I submit that this gap is a risk which must
be taken in a free society. We cannot afford to dis-

miss the human element in decision-making where
basic liberties are at stake.

ᕯᕢ

The whole process [of lie-detector tests] smacks
of twentieth-century witchcraft. Does the flesh of
the applicant burn when a hot iron is applied to it?
When tightly bound and thrown into a pond, does
the applicant sink or float? When strapped in a
chair with electrodes and other gadgets attached,
does the rate of respiration and blood pressure of
the applicant rise? Does the salt of his pores induce
increased electrical conductivity? Are we reduced
to alchemy as a technique of screening applicants
for highly sensitive positions in the Federal bureaucracy?

ᕯᕢ

I lost my faith in the infallibility of the computer
when the Social Security Administration sent me a
check for $754 and some cents covered by a state-
ment that they had determined I was entitled to
lump sum death benefits. So I sent them the check
back with a statement that I was very glad to be
able to report to them that any data which they had
in their computer that indicated that I had passed
into the great beyond had been very slightly exaggerated.

ᕯᕢ

Ironically, it is our progress that has produced our
problem. Progress is something we all admire and
strive to achieve; but, like the law, it must evolve

naturally, with adequate time for men to adjust to it, or it can become the master rather than the servant.

This relentless drive to overcome the barriers of nature has created our great modern technology. But the very technology it has created seems apt to destroy our civilization.

FREEDOM

Sam Ervin knows freedom is hard won and easily lost. His guardianship of individual liberties is the first line of defense against incursion by bureaucrats flying the banner of efficiency, politicians in the vanguard of special interests, and zealots who would deny to others the rights they insist upon for themselves. To Sam Ervin, freedom for all is more than just a line in the Pledge of Allegiance—it is the common denominator in the formula for democracy.

The bigger a government grows, the smaller the people grow.

❧

America must choose between equality coerced by law and freedom of the individual. She cannot have both. As for me, I choose freedom of the individual as the more precious of these incompatible things.

❧

The Founding Fathers discovered this shocking, but everlasting, truth: nothing short of tyranny can quench the insatiable thirst of government for power; in its ardor to expand and multiply its authority, government will extinguish the freedom of the individual, unless it is restrained from doing so by fundamental law which it alone can neither repeal nor amend.

∞

A freedom sacrificed is seldom resurrected.

∞

SENATOR ERVIN: Do you agree with me that the First Amendment grants its freedoms to all persons within the boundaries of our country?

WITNESS: Yes.

SENATOR ERVIN: And that, consequently, it grants its freedoms to both the wise and the foolish?

WITNESS: Yes.

SENATOR ERVIN: The profound and the shallow?

WITNESS: Yes.

SENATOR ERVIN: The devout and the ungodly? And those that hate our country and its institutions as well as those who love our country and its institutions?

WITNESS: Yes, I do.

SENATOR ERVIN: And do you agree with me that until the mere expression of ideas ceases and crime ensues that the best interests of our country are served by recognizing the fact that the First Amendment protects the utterances of all kinds and conditions of men?

WITNESS: Yes, sir.

SENATOR ERVIN: I thank you for a very interesting statement.

ᙅᙆᙅ

First Amendment freedoms are often grossly abused. Society is sorely tempted at times to demand or countenance their curtailment by government to prevent abuse. Our country must steadfastly spurn this temptation if it is to remain the land of the free. This is so partly because the only way to prevent the abuse of freedom is to abolish freedom.

ᙅᙆᙅ

If it is justified, protest may lead to reform; and if it is unjustified, protest may relieve at least temporarily the tensions of the protesters. In either event, protest has therapeutic value for both protesters and society.

ᙅᙆᙅ

Besides, a free and full interchange of ideas concerning the problems of government and society make us aware of conditions and policies which need correction, and induces us to make in apt time and in a peaceful way the reforms that changing times demand. As a consequence, violent revolution has no rational or rightful place in our system.

ᙅᙆᙅ

Since the doctrine of civil disobedience is invoked with such frequency nowadays, it seems not amiss to emphasize that the Constitution does not countenance civil disobedience which contemplates and produces unlawful acts.

Government has an inherent right to self-protection, and may under some conditions prohibit or punish the advocacy or teaching of the desirability of overthrowing it by violent means.

༄

After all, the first duty of a free society is to enforce law and thus maintain order. This is so because disorder denies the people the right to exercise and enjoy their freedoms.

༄

The Founding Fathers rightly believed that truth alone makes men free. They desired most of all that the people for whom they were creating a government should be politically, intellectually, and spiritually free.

In the nature of things, they could not guarantee that Americans would actually know the truth. But they could guarantee that Americans would have the right to know the truth, and make that right effective by conferring upon the people and denying to the government the power to determine what truth is.

༄

Freedom of thought and speech are the things which distinguish our country most sharply from totalitarian regimes. They enable our country to enjoy a diversity of ideas and programs, and to escape the standardization of ideas and programs totalitarian tyranny requires.

༄

The First Amendment protects all utterances, individual or concerted, advocating constitutional or political changes, however revolutionary they may be, if the utterances contemplate that the changes are to be achieved by lawful means. Hence, freedom of speech permits an individual or a group to advocate the adoption of communism, fascism, or any other system of government by means of the ballot box.

つ〜つ

The best test of truth is its ability to get itself accepted when conflicting ideas compete for the minds of men. The Founding Fathers staked the existence of America as a free society upon their faith that it has nothing to fear from the exercise of First Amendment freedoms, no matter how much they may be abused, as long as it leaves truth free to combat error.

つ〜つ

Strange as it may seem, freedom has many foes, even among those who profess to love it. Some men are annoyed by the abuse of freedom by others and advocate its abridgment to prevent further abuse. Other men fear the exercise of freedom by others and demand its curtailment to quiet their fears.

And government itself tends to dislike freedom in general because it obstructs the exercise of arbitrary power, and freedom of speech and of the press in particular because they are the instruments which expose official mismanagement and misconduct.

つ〜つ

The foes of freedom never tire. Consequently, freedom is always in jeopardy.

∽

Lovers of liberty have learned that they must secure freedom from subtle dangers as well as from its avowed enemies. We must not forget that the First Amendment was meant to protect freedom for the weak and cowardly as well as for the strong and courageous.

∽

Since so many men now appear to swap the reality of human liberty for the mirage of economic security, it would be well if we would pause a moment and ponder the choice our ancestors made when they forsook the comparative security of the Old World for the terrifying insecurity of the New. It was not without many pangs of regret that they turned their backs for all time upon the scenes of their childhood, the graves of their beloved dead, the comparative security of the then-civilized world, and journeyed in tiny barks across a boisterous ocean to establish homes for themselves and their children and their children's children in what was then a perilous wilderness in a new and strange land.

Why did they do this? Why did they exchange the comparative security of the Old World for the terrifying insecurity of the New? The answer is simply this and nothing more: they believed that only the slave, who depends upon a master for the bread of bondage, is really secure; and they knew that only the self-reliant soul, who spurns security for opportunity, is truly free. For this reason, they chose liberty rather than security.

༄

The brave men and women who brought the love of liberty to these shores did not learn economics sitting at the feet of those who promise "abundance for all by robbing Selected Peter to pay Collective Paul." They acquired their knowledge the hard way. Their teachers were despotic governments, which robbed them of the fruits of their labor by confiscatory taxation, and in that way reduced them to the status of economic slaves.

༄

Liberty reveals herself in a threefold guise as economic liberty, political liberty, and religious liberty.

༄

Much has been said recently concerning "human rights" as opposed to "property rights." This is nonsense. Property has no rights, only attributes. The right to property is a human right, a civil right—a right expressly protected by the Constitution. It is one of the basic rights of a free people. Conversely, failure to protect the human right to property is a typical characteristic of totalitarian states along with the denial of freedom of speech, press, and religion.

༄

The freedom to own property and to control the property one owns is essential in very large degree to the enjoyment of any other freedom.

∽

The principle that "every man's home is his castle" is more than a slogan. It is an expression of one of the greatest longings of the human heart. The longing for a place where a man can flee from the world, where he can converse freely with his family, and his God, free from the fear of molestation by others or by his government. In the words of the Prophet Micah: "But they shall sit every man under his vine and under his fig tree; and none shall make them afraid: for the mouth of the Lord of Hosts has spoken it."

∽

I used to have some difficulty in understanding exactly what Thomas Jefferson meant in speaking of the pursuit of happiness, but it seems to me that the only way we can pursue happiness is in an atmosphere of freedom and an atmosphere in which we can have a right of privacy in those areas of life which I think we are entitled to keep free from governmental interference. I think that is what the idea was. They might not have phrased it that way, but the Declaration of Independence and the Bill of Rights certainly indicate that the Founding Fathers appreciated you couldn't pursue happiness unless you had freedom.

∽

The most vital legacy we share is our notion of the dignity of the individual and his freedom of conscience—his liberty to speak, act, and think for himself without coercion of any sort. Any practice, any act, any threat which reduces a man in dignity, which limits the freedom of his conscience or his capacity for thinking and acting for himself—this is wrong, whether it be termed an invasion of his privacy or tyranny over his mind.

∽

Knowledge that the government is engaged in surveillance of its citizens creates an atmosphere of fear which is inimical to freedom. It stifles political discussion and leads to a cowed and subservient population which does not dare disagree with government policy or accepted wisdom. Democracy cannot survive if the people are sullen, scared, or rebellious.

∽

I just don't see much difference between keeping information on a man and having him under surveillance. I think the difference between them is not nearly as great as the difference between Tweedledum and Tweedledee.

∽

I am constantly amazed at the broad range of excuses and reasons for intrusive surveys and collection of personal data, for coercive practices affecting the liberties of [Federal] employees as citizens.

For instance, every few months, they force an employee to disclose his creditors, assets, and liabilities, including how much cash he has in his safe-deposit boxes, and they plead "prevention of conflict of interest." They ask him whether he likes tall girls, whether he loves his mother, or if he likes poetry, and they plead "mental health" or "emotional stability."

They require supervisors to conduct surveys of pregnancy of female employees and they cite "fire drills" as a reason.

They require college students applying for summer jobs to submit to interviews about their dating habits and they plead "national security."

If he responds to those government questionnaires, "I can't answer," or "I won't answer," the computer responds, "You will," and the supervisor adds, "Or else!"

༒

. . . It became alarmingly clear that the Federal government was bent on setting itself up as the "Great Protector" of the personal habits, thoughts, actions, and emotions of its vast work-force. This overprotectiveness and "Big-Brotherism" of the government has led it to devise ingenious means to rob employees of the American dream of freedom. . . . Here are examples of some questions employees are asked to answer with the response of "true" or "false":

> I have never indulged in any unusual sex practices.
>
> I am a special agent of God.
>
> I loved my mother.
>
> I hated my father.

I was often sent to the principal's office, as a
child, for misconduct.

I am often bothered by a tenderness on the top
of my head.

Now, I don't mind having my wife ask me if I
love her, but I would resent having to tell an in-
quisitive bureaucrat whether I am bothered by a
tenderness on the top of my head.

∽

Coercion of Federal employees to buy United
States savings bonds and to contribute to charities
became a source of particular concern. We received
thousands of complaints indicating that the "vol-
untariness" of the savings-bond and charitable-
contribution drives was only an empty word. [We]
even discovered that men in Vietnam fighting from
foxholes were "asked" to "support their government" by buying savings bonds. I should think that
weathering a storm of bullets is the supreme expression of support for one's country.

∽

We have evidence that on one occasion out in
Colorado, there were 119 people present at a rally
to protest the war in Vietnam, and that of those 119
persons, 52 of them were military intelligence agents.
Not only that, but a military intelligence agent was
sent with orders to tape the speeches that were made
at the rally and he couldn't tape them because the
military forces had five helicopters flying right over
the heads of the rally and making so much noise
that the speeches that were made could not be taped.

∽

There are many other privacy-invading devices about which I could speak at length—for instance, lie detectors, loyalty oaths, probing personnel forms, restrictions on communicating with members of Congress, and pressures to support political parties financially.

However, one device in particular deserves special attention. Wiretapping, that sneaky business that has become a plaything in America—especially in the government—during the past few years, has become a term on the tongue of every American. . . . I have become convinced that its rampant use is not consonant with a free society.

∽

These practices affect not only [a citizen's] right to speak and act according to the dictates of his conscience, they invade also his right not to speak at all, not to act at all, and not to participate at all. In today's society, with the world becoming, according to Mr. McLuhan, "a global village," this may well be the most precious right enjoyed by civilized man.

The Federal Constitution specifically protects him in the enjoyment of these rights. If the Federal government itself will not respect these sacred rights, how can it be expected private parties will do so? You, as young lawyers, are the logical guardians of this right that Emily Dickinson would call the right to be "Nobody." Guard it well.

∽

There are fashions in follies as in everything else, and I think we have tolerated long enough the current fashions in privacy invasion. In the name of social experiment, in the cause of management efficiency, in behalf of technological advances and scientific research, we have too long permitted Americans to be subjected to practices and devices which should have no place in a society of free men.

∽

We are not powerless to fight the invasions of our privacy, incursions on our liberties, or the dangers inherent in the trend to complete computerization. The resources of our constitutional heritage provide our ammunition.

∽

There are many restrictions on American citizens. But I do not think that is a very valid argument for imposing more restrictions on him and robbing him of more liberties.

∽

There is no clear line between freedom and repression. Freedom is a fluid, intangible condition of our society. It thrives at some periods and is beset at others. It is lost not all at a time, but by degrees.

∽

The tides of fear are rising, and the anchors of faith are dragging. It is in such a time frightened humanity needs freedom most.

Since courage is better than fear, and faith is better than doubt, let us spurn fear, cherish faith, and dedicate ourselves to this proposition: Freedom is life's supreme value and must be preserved for ourselves and our posterity, cost what it may.

SENATORS AND THE SENATE

Sam Ervin has enlivened Senate debate with his pungent wit since 1954 when his North Carolina stories in the censure debate on the conduct of Joseph McCarthy struck to the very heart of the issue so crisply that no one could possibly misunderstand what was involved. When arguments become heated and verbiage and sophistry obscure the issue, he can usually be counted on to restore focus and to temper anger with an appropriate tale which both amuses and informs.

On one occasion the following question was put to Dr. Hale: "Doctor, when you pray as Chaplain of the Senate, do you look at the tragic condition of the country and the many problems existing in the country and then pray that the Almighty will give the Senators the wisdom to deal with these problems and to find their solutions?"

In reply to that interrogation, Dr. Hale said, "No,

I do not look at the country and pray for the Senators. I look at the Senators and pray for the country."

෨෨

Sometimes I think it would be a good thing to have a constitutional provision that says no fool can be a member of the U.S. Senate.

෨෨

The proposal that we have a moratorium instead of a total end to busing our little children to achieve racial balance reminds me of the story of the man who wanted a short-tailed dog. To that end, he cut off his dog's tail just a little bit at a time so, as he said, he wouldn't hurt the dog too much. If the dog's tail—that is, the busing of children for integration purposes—should be cut off, it should be cut off all at once. We should not leave the question to be debated and argued again.

෨෨

If I may change the metaphor, the proponents of a change in the rules were saying, in effect, that the Senate was like Josh Billings's mule: "It didn't kick according to no rules," and the reason why the Senate could not act was, like Josh Billings's mule, the Senate had no rules.

෨෨

They tell a story about the British flier whose plane came down in Ireland during the Second World War. Ireland, of course, was not engaged in the war. An Irish policeman arrested the British pilot but then permitted him to go. The policeman's superior officer found out that the policeman had arrested the pilot and then released him.

Said the superior officer to the policeman, "You should not have released him. Don't you know that Ireland is neutral?"

The policeman replied, "Yes, but I know which side we are neutral on."

It is the same with this bill: the Federal government, the administration, and the advocates of this bill are neutral on the side of the plaintiff in the suits to be brought under the bill.

∽

Mr. President, the argument of my good friend from Maine that what this amendment is designed to accomplish has already been accomplished by the Byrd amendment, reminds me of the story of the man in a distant part of the country who received a telegram from an undertaker informing him that his mother-in-law had died. The telegram of the undertaker closed with the inquiry, "Shall we cremate or bury?"

The man wired back and said, "Take no chances. Cremate and bury."

∽

If the Constitution required air conditioning to be cut out in the Capitol and the Senate Office Building and the House Office Building, I would quit.

∽

The amendment of the distinguished Senator from Delaware reminds me of the fisherman who went fishing and carried his frying pan with him. He caught a little fish and wanted to fry the fish while it was fresh. He got out his knife and started to disembowel the fish. The fish kept fighting and resisting, and the fisherman said to the fish, "I don't see why you're struggling so much against me. All I want to do is gut you."

That is precisely what the Roth amendment would do to this bill.

∽

When I entered the Senate chamber on Monday, I felt as though I had stepped through the looking glass. After only one hour of debate, it was announced that what is reputed to be the greatest deliberative body in the world would be asked to gag itself. Today we will vote on that resolution, and I trust that it will be defeated overwhelmingly.

∽

Despite my great affection for the Vice President, I am constrained to observe that his proposed ruling reminds me of a story. On one occasion, a gentleman whom I shall call Hubert was walking along a public street. He was wearing a sweater which had a big letter K emblazoned on its front. Hubert met a friend whom I shall call Frank. Frank stopped Hubert and put this inquiry to him:

"What does the big letter K mean?"

Hubert replied, "It means I am confused."

Frank, who was very much gifted in the use of the

English language, thereupon said, "Hubert, you don't spell 'confused' with a K."

Hubert replied, "If you are as confused as I am, you do."

∽

I would say, Senator, that there is about as much similarity between this proposal and the man who works as a welder as there is between the flowers that bloom in the spring, tra-la, and the nightshirt of the Emperor of Japan.

∽

Mr. President, the committee that has acted on this bill has about as much jurisdiction over this matter as I have to select underwear for the Queen of Sheba. For that reason, I move that the bill be committed to the Senate Committee on the Judiciary.

∽

You know, the Scriptures speak about the man who sowed seed on stony ground, and I would have to speak of the Senate, which is noteworthy at this moment for the absence of Senators, as being stony ground. I do not care to talk too much longer on this subject for that reason.

∽

. . . I thought they would be present to hear something about these bills. But I have decided that they are all like the old justice of the peace down in North Carolina who had the misfortune of having to try a lawsuit in which two lawyers appeared on opposite sides on the day he wanted to go fishing. When they got through taking the evidence, the justice of the peace asked the lawyers if they wanted to argue the case, and they said yes, they wanted to argue the case. Then he asked them how much time they wanted to argue, and they said an hour on each side. He told them they had that right. He said, "But I have to go fishing. You can proceed with the argument. I will go fishing. When you finish with the argument, look under this book on my desk. You will see that I have the decision already written out."

I do not charge that Senators who are now locked in the embrace of Morpheus have actually written out their decisions, because I hope they will be willing to receive more light.

∽

Like the Scripture says, "men love the days rather than the nights." I prefer not to go into night sessions.

∽

I fear that some members of the Senate may be in need of psychiatric treatment. We are here tonight not because the Senator from South Carolina wants to make a speech, but because the Democratic leadership of the Senate, in effect, is aiding and abetting the Republican leadership of the Senate to compel us, against our will, to speak against a Republican so-called civil-rights bill advocated by the Republican administration.

I do not know whether the Senator from South Carolina agrees with me, but this situation reminds me of the lecturer who delivered a lecture entitled, "Why Are We Here?" It was a very fine lecture, and the superintendent of a hospital for mental defectives heard him deliver it. He thought it had some fine therapeutic qualities that would be beneficial to the inmates of his institution, so the superintendent of the hospital for mental defectives invited the lecturer to come and deliver the lecture to the inmates of his institution. The lecturer rose and started the speech in his usual way. He asked, "Why are we here?"

One of the inmates of the institution rose and said, "You asked a simple question—'Why are we here?' We are here because we are not all there," pointing to his head.

 perspiring

Despite my good relations with my good friend, the Senator from Wyoming, I am going to say that he is the mildest-mannered man that ever scuttled a ship or cut a throat or usurped a power that he did not possess.

 perspiring

This chart showing the requests for rate increases pending reminds me of a colloquy between George and his friend Bill. George said, "Bill, my wife is the most extravagant woman; she is always wanting fifty cents for this and fifty cents for that and fifty cents for this other thing." And Bill said, "What does she do with all that money?" George said, "She doesn't get it."

perspiring

. . . The overwhelming majority of Congressmen will undoubtedly support the measure. Consequently, I have been strongly tempted to disobey the injunction of Exodus 23:2, which says: "Thou shall not follow a multitude to do evil," and vote for the bill. To enable myself to do this, I had hoped that I might find a spiritual surgeon who would amputate my conscience, and permit me to vote for a politically popular bill which is fraught with great peril to the future of my country.

I have not been able to find a spiritual surgeon to amputate my conscience. For this reason I cannot vote for the revenue-sharing bill.

ᖌᐡ

Crime and dangerous drugs present hard problems. Hard problems are the quicksands of sound legislation.

ᖌᐡ

. . . The Senator from North Carolina, for one, is not willing to reach a conclusion that the creek is dry unless the Senator from North Carolina first goes and takes a look at the creek and, if there is any water there, takes a wade in it a little bit.

SENATOR SCOTT: All I can say is the Senator has a very long pole.

SENATOR ERVIN: My experience has been that it takes a long pole to reach some things.

SENATOR SCOTT: That is entirely too dangerous to pursue further.

SENATOR ERVIN: Yes, because we may get drowned in the dry creek.

ᖌᐡ

I think there were two motives that prompted the House amendments. I should not say this about my fellow members of Congress—but one was a motive to work both sides of the street, and the other was to get a camel's nose under the tent this time so that the whole camel and all of the camel's family could come under next time.

∽

One time when I was a member of the North Carolina Legislature, I got a petition signed by fifteen people asking me to pass a law repealing all the loopholes in the law.

∽

SENATOR MORSE: I suggested, earlier in my speech today, that I would be delighted to enlist in the rear ranks of the army under the captaincy or generalship of the distinguished Senator from Alabama or the distinguished Senator from Tennessee. I have urged them to take the leading position in this band, and to stand under the motto, "It Shall Not Pass."

SENATOR ERVIN: Mr. President, will the Senator from Oregon yield for a question?

SENATOR MORSE: I yield for a question.

SENATOR ERVIN: I wish to ask my distinguished friend, the Senator from Oregon, whether the army of which he is speaking is engaged in a gas attack.

∽

They are in a big hurry to pass this bill, so they say. It reminds me, with all due respect to my brethren who advocate this bill, of a story of Irvin S.

Cobb. He went into this store to buy a necktie. They offered to sell him a very loud necktie, and he pushed it away saying he did not want that kind of necktie. And the clerk kept trying to sell him that particular necktie. Finally Irvin S. Cobb said:

"I do not want that tie. I would not be caught wearing it down in the bottom of a coal mine at twelve o'clock midnight during a total eclipse of the moon while John L. Lewis and the United Mine Workers were out on strike."

Now, I do not blame them for wanting to pass this bill. But I would not want to be caught with this bill in my possession down in the bottom of a coal mine at twelve o'clock midnight during a total eclipse of the moon while John L. Lewis and the United Mine Workers are out on strike.

∽

In my opinion it is far better that no bill be passed than one which is ill-conceived and ill-considered.

∽

Despite the fact that some of these projections and estimates that are made are final, I will tell another story to illustrate something about estimates.

Bill asked his friend George, "What became of your old hound dog?"

He said, "I sold him for five thousand dollars."

Bill said, "George, you know you never got five thousand dollars for that old hound dog."

He said, "No, I did not get it in cash, but I got it in trade. I took two alley cats which were estimated to be worth two thousand, five hundred dollars apiece."

I think it is pretty bad when a law comes along and says estimates and projections are going to be final and not open to question.

∽

It will not make a particle of difference. However, the story relates that a man applied for a job to teach geography in school. There was an argument at the time as to whether the world was flat or round. The school board was divided on that proposition. The man came before the school board and was asked what position he held. He said, "I leave that up to the school board. I teach either theory."

That is the reason that I am hesitant to accept the interpretation put on the amendment by my good friend, because his interpretations sort of vary and perambulate from one point of view to another point of view. Mine never change.

∽

The Senator from Indiana is like the man who says he does not believe everything he reads in the Bible, that he does not believe Jonah swallowed the whale.

∽

Now, it grieves me very much to disagree with my friend from Massachusetts. He complained that he thought you were somewhat immoderate in your statement.

I have read your statement and I have read the

House amendments. And I am not comparing you with Warren Hastings, but having read this statement and the amendments, I am reminded of the story of what Warren Hastings said when he was impeached as the Governor General of India for money he had extorted by bribes and larceny from the people of India. He said in defense that, when he considered how great the opportunities were that he had to steal money and how little he had stolen, he was surprised at his own moderation. After reading the House amendments to Title VI and reading and hearing your statement, I am surprised at your moderation.

∞

Thomas Jefferson asked George Washington why the Convention had created the Senate, instead of reposing all legislative power in the House of Representatives. George Washington replied, "The Convention created the Senate in order that it might do the same thing your saucer is doing. You are cooling off your hot coffee in your saucer. The Constitutional Convention created the Senate in order that the hot legislation passed by the House might be cooled before it is poured down the throats of the people of America."

∞

SENATOR RUSSELL LONG: Can the Senator explain why anyone would be so zealous as to the rights of a minority group in a distant state that they would not want to permit their own minority groups to have the same benefits?

SENATOR ERVIN: Two things account for that. One is that it is not politically profitable to do any reform at home. Another is that if a man looks at the supposed sins of someone way off somewhere it acts as a sort of opium and blinds him to the sins on his own doorstep.

∽

A little over one hundred years ago my state attempted to leave the Union, and the Union said:

"You cannot do that; you cannot get out of the Union."

We found we could not get out of the Union. But we have also been trying to get back into the Union, and we cannot get back into the Union.

I have some amendments to get North Carolina back into the Union.

∽

This is a very simple amendment. While I would not under any circumstances be willing to remove permanently from North Carolina, even to go to the Kingdom of Heaven, if I could get there, this is one time when I wish I could temporarily move my residence north of the Mason-Dixon line, because if I did, I am sure the Senate would adopt this amendment.

∽

I might say that the right to privacy has been close to my heart since my first days in the Senate when I was appointed a member of the special committee to investigate the late Senator McCarthy.

Assuredly that assignment was no easy task, but those trying times firmly convinced me that about the most important thing a man has is his right to privacy and to individual dignity. During that unfortunate era of fear and whispering those two concepts found themselves, like the whooping crane, near extinction.

∽

Mr. President, many years ago there was a custom in a section of my country, known as the South Mountains, to hold religious meetings at which the oldest members of the congregation were called upon to stand up and publicly testify to their religious experiences. On one occasion they were holding such a meeting in one of their churches, and old Uncle Ephraim Swink, a South Mountaineer whose body was all bent and distorted with arthritis, was present. All the older members of the congregation except Uncle Ephraim arose and gave testimony to their religious experiences. Uncle Ephraim kept his seat. Thereupon, the moderator said, "Brother Ephraim, suppose you tell us what the Lord has done for you."

Uncle Ephraim rose, with his bent and distorted body, and said, "Brother, He has mighty nigh ruint me."

Mr. President, that is about what Senator [Joseph] McCarthy has done to the Senate.

∽

How are we going to enhance the respect which the people of the United States, so we think, ought to have for the Senate of the United States, when the Senate emulates the example of the old doctor who prescribed medicine for his patients which he would not take himself?

ᙄᙄ

It is a custom in this country to solve most of the problems by majority rule. I ought to be opposed to majority rule because I have died from more lost causes than any other member of the Senate. However, it is still the only way decisions can be made.

The minority has the opportunity to exercise wisdom and convince the majority of the rectitude of its cause. But the decision has to be made by the majority.

CRIME AND PUNISHMENT

Sam Ervin holds that while the accused is always entitled to a fair trial, the victims of crime and society are just as much entitled to justice as the accused. He believes the speedy and fair administration of justice to inflict certain and reasonable punishment to those guilty of criminal activity is the best means of ensuring law and order. To this end, he has authored much of the most progressive and significant federal crime legislation of the past two decades.

. . . I will tell you a story about a person being a victim of circumstantial evidence.

Johnny loved blackberry jam and was always stealing blackberry jam. His mother told him if she ever caught him stealing any more blackberry jam she would give him hail Columbia.

Johnny behaved for several days until finally the temptation was too great, and he got ahold of a jar of blackberry jam and got to eating it, which he en-

97

joyed. After a while, he got too much and his stomach began hurting him and then his conscience bothered him, and he was afraid that he would be given hail Columbia.

He caught the tomcat there around the house and spread the blackberry jam around the cat's face. After awhile his mother came in and saw the blackberry jam jar about empty and the blackberry jam all over the cat's face. When Johnny's father came home, she told him about it, and his father got the tomcat in one hand and the shotgun in the other and went down in the woods behind the house, and in a few minutes, Johnny heard the shotgun fired and said, "Poor old tomcat, a victim of circumstantial evidence."

So there you are.

∽

Fallible human beings have to administer justice, and I sometimes think that if we get close enough to touch the hem of Justice's garment, then we are doing a pretty good job.

∽

It seems to me if you can say any function of our judicial system is more sacred than another it is the function of the administration of criminal justice.

∽

It is indeed a pathetic commentary on the criminal-justice system in our country that more than half of the inmates in city and county jails across the nation are imprisoned without having been convicted of a crime.

෮ඟ

One of the deficiencies which is responsible in large measure for crime is the fact that our prison system tends to be a postgraduate course in crime.

෮ඟ

When I was practicing law, I often had clients convicted for various offenses and sentenced to serve in the penitentiary. On one occasion, I received a letter from one of these clients after he had been serving a short while. By his letter he implored me to see the governor and obtain a pardon for him. He gave me as the reason for his request that there were many bad and disreputable men in the penitentiary and he didn't want to associate with them.

෮ඟ

Of course, we could prevent crime outside prison by putting everybody in prison.

෮ඟ

I fear that there is more truth than fiction in the observation that tall prison walls better serve to keep outsiders from seeing the injustice within than to prevent the individuals within from fleeing or harming society.

෮ඟ

Justice is supposed to be blind, but it is not supposed to be deaf to testimony.

ᴖᴑ

We had a justice of the peace in North Carolina who had been newly appointed to office and in his first case a defendant was brought before him on a criminal charge.

The J.P. said, "Are you guilty or not guilty?"

The defendant said, "I'm not guilty."

The J.P. said, "Go about your business. If you are not guilty, you have no business here."

The constable said to the J.P., "You ought to hear the witness for the prosecution before you tell the man to go."

And the J.P. said, "He said he is not guilty, and therefore I am not going to investigate this matter any further."

ᴖᴑ

One of the best ways to reduce crime is to enforce law in such a way that people believe that the law is fair, and that results in respect for the law.

ᴖᴑ

When people get righteously concerned about things such as today's cry of law and order, they are likely to do some very unwise things.

ᴖᴑ

False claims that necessity justifies tampering or infringing or suspending constitutional guarantees in the name of law and order or security should be

rejected whenever they are offered. If we are willing
to sacrifice hard-won freedom in a vain search for
security, we will no doubt find ourselves with neither
liberty or security.

∞

To my mind, trying to deal with the crime problem by preventive detention is just about as wise as
trying to empty the Atlantic Ocean with a quart cup.

∞

The most immediate way to deal with the problem
of crime is to have courts sufficient to give a speedy
trial to those charged with crime and to inflict a
certain and speedy but reasonable punishment on
those who are convicted.

∞

A friend of mine was a candidate for Congress and
had a number of moonshiners whom he was retained
to defend before Judge Webb back in my district in
North Carolina. Judge Webb called him up and said,
"I know you are running for Congress and I know
you would rather get out to campaign than try your
cases in court so I will continue your cases until the
next term of court."

My friend said he got his clients together and told
them that the judge would continue their cases if
they wished. One of the old moonshiners said, "I
want mine continued."

The lawyer said, "I don't know why you want it
continued. You were caught red-handed at the still;

you have no defense; you might as well dispose of it and get it behind you."

The old moonshiner said, "I don't feel that way about it. I would like to have it continued. I might be lucky and die before the trial."

∽

The lesson we should have learned long before now on the need for speedy justice was stated many centuries ago by Ecclesiastes, the preacher, when he said:

"Because sentence against an evil deed is not executed speedily, the heart of the sons of men is fully set to do evil."

∽

We had a prosecuting attorney in my state named Moss, and once in a term of court every one of the defendants was acquitted and he got to the last case and the defense lawyer quoted that it is better for nine guilty men to escape than for one innocent man to be convicted. When Moss got up he said, "The trouble with that is, ninety-nine have already escaped." I have great faith in the American system of justice based upon the fact that when lawyers undertake to defend people, they are so faithful to their professional obligations that I think it is very rare when a man feels that innocent people are often convicted.

∽

When a man commits a serious crime, that crime preys upon his mind and if he has got a conscience it also preys upon his conscience. A man usually finds some relief in talking about what is preying upon his mind.

❧

There is an old saying that a man very rarely regrets saying too little.

❧

A lot of my clients were convicted because they did not have sense enough to take my advice and keep their mouths shut.

❧

I always found my clients who were moonshiners to be very honorable men and very law-abiding in all respects except when it came to making moonshine.

There is a Judge Webb in North Carolina and there were also two boys down in Wilkes County who also had the name Webb, and whom I have known over many years. They make moonshine whiskey, go to prison for a while, go home, go back to making whiskey again, and come back to prison. So I say we have grown up together, so to speak.

I talked with Judge Webb about them and told him that I had made a proposal to them. I once told them that I had a private foundation that would grant them a living wage, if only they would agree not to go into manufacturing whiskey again. And they said they didn't want anything to do with "store-bought whiskey" and couldn't accept such a proposal. I said, "You think it over and I will put you in touch with this private charity that I know."

Well, they said, "We will think it over." So, I came back later and I said, "Will you accept my proposition?" They said, "No, we can't accept your proposition." They just didn't want to be dependent upon anybody. They didn't want to live off the labor of somebody else.

If they hadn't had a great strength of intellectual honesty they would have accepted the offer of a living wage, even if they had no intention of complying with the conditions of it.

ᘒ

My experience—and I have spent some time in the courtroom—has led me to the conclusion that when a man says one thing one time and another later you do not know which time to believe, even if you believe he is telling the truth one time.

ᘒ

We discover truth in fragments and must piece it together like a picture puzzle.

ᘒ

This analysis of various conversations convinces me that Lord Coke was right when he said that the scratch of a pen is worth the slippery memory of many witnesses. It calls to mind one of the first cases in which I participated. My client was charged with murdering his wife by stabbing her in the neck. Four witnesses appeared at the trial and testified that they had gone to the jail together and each one had asked my client whether he had killed his wife. The first witness said my client did not say anything, but that he shook his head no. The second witness said that my client answered the question with a simple yes and nothing else. The third witness said that my client had said "Yes," but that it was an accident. The fourth witness said that my client had said, "Yes, I took the knife and jabbed it in her throat." So, I still have a very profound conviction that Lord Coke was right.

∽

The truth is the truth whether it is told under oath or not.

∽

You could just do away with laws creating crimes and thereby reduce the crime rate most remarkably.

∽

Instead of clamoring after panaceas offered in the name of law and order, it would be better to address ourselves to the slow, hard, and expensive course of improving and reforming our criminal-justice system.

∽

The twin evils of criminal and political violence stand as a threat to our liberty in two ways. Liberty cannot survive in anarchy. But neither can it survive if our nation's leaders and people come to feel that the only path to security lies in suspending constitutional freedoms "for the duration."

∽

If America is to be free, her government must permit her people to think their own thoughts and determine their own associations without official instruction or intimidation; and if America is to be secure, her Government must punish her people, not for the thoughts they think or the associations they choose, but only for the crimes they commit.

∾

Several years ago an old counterfeiter, who was counterfeiting one-dollar bills, was up for trial, after spending only a few of them. The judge pointed out to him, when he came up for trial, that he had a great record of service in the Navy and had been decorated and was eligible for a pension of sixty dollars per month. He told the judge, "I have been saving the Government money. I have not been passing off more than twenty-five or thirty of the counterfeit dollars a month."

Then they read the indictment which said that the people of the United States of America were against him, and he said, "If all of the people of the United States of America are against me, Judge, then I am ready to go to jail now."

THE PRESS

Sam Ervin has great confidence in the judgment of the American people and is certain that they will ultimately make the right decisions if they have full access to the facts. He views a free press, constantly probing the bureaucratic bastions of government, as a potent antidote to government's insatiable thirst for power and its propensity to abuse it. Therefore, he has steadfastly defended the right of the press to provide the people with the facts and has fiercely fought all attempts by government to limit its right to inquiry, intimidate it, or muzzle it.

I have always believed in freedom of information, whether the news is good or bad.

∞

I guess I am one of the few men in political life who doesn't complain much about his treatment at the hands of the press. The press takes me to task

107

every once in awhile, but they have always been very kind, not attributing my hypocrisy to bad motives. They have always attributed it to a lack of mental capacity.

⚭

I think reporters are pretty well trained to ask questions which are both pertinent and impertinent.

⚭

Undoubtedly there are a lot of good men in the press.

⚭

There are also people in the press, just like there are in the Senate and House and every other profession, that abuse the great power of the press.

⚭

Nobody has ever been smart enough yet to extend the freedom of the press to the wise and just members of the fourth estate and deny it to members of the fourth estate who may be unwise and unjust.

⚭

Our Founding Fathers were wise enough to know that there is no way to give freedom of speech and press to the wise and deny it to fools and knaves. Certainly, they did not intend for the government to decide who were the wise and who were the fools and who were the knaves.

⚭

I am a great believer in the freedom of the press for all purposes, not only the chastisement of politicians. I would even go so far in defense of the free press as to say what Samson said about Jehovah: "Though he slay me, yet I praise him."

ᴄᴧᴐ

It is easier to suggest than to appraise the value of a free press to a free nation. Thomas Jefferson did this in a trenchant manner when he said, "Were it left to me to decide whether we should have a government without newspapers, or newspapers without a government, I should not hesitate a moment to prefer the latter."

ᴄᴧᴐ

Freedom of the press does not exist for the benefit of newspapers. To be sure, newspapers are the merchandisers of the news. They are actuated by the profit motive in gathering, printing, and commenting upon current events, and it is to be hoped that they find these endeavors to be profitable undertakings. I repeat, however, that freedom of the press does not exist for the benefit of newspapers.

ᴄᴧᴐ

Freedom of the press exists in America for the benefit of all of the people of America. The validity of this observation is obvious if due heed is paid to these facts: First, an informed and unprejudiced electorate is essential to the existence of a democracy; and, second, a proper free press is a prerequisite to an informed and unprejudiced electorate. It is no exaggeration to say that we must have a free press if we are to have a free nation.

∞

Josh Billings was right when he declared that "it is better to be ignorant than to know what ain't so." It is essential for newspapers to serve the cause of truth in gathering and printing the news and the cause of fairness in commenting upon it if we are to have an informed and unprejudiced rather than a misinformed and prejudiced citizenship in our nation.

∞

There are some people, not including me, who think that the press is sometimes like Providence. Down in North Carolina, this Pennsylvania Dutchman had a gristmill on the Yadkin River, and the rains descended and the floods came and it washed his gristmill away. He walked up to the top of the hill overlooking the river to see what havoc had been wrought and he saw his mill had been washed away. And he said, taking Providence up one side and down the other: "It does just about as much harm as it does good."

Some folks say the same thing about newspapers.

∞

It sometimes appears that some government officials assume the role of the press is to present news about government policies and action only in the best possible light. And it sometimes appears that some members of the press unjustifiably interpret

THE WISDOM OF SAM ERVIN 111

any official response to their criticism, other than acquiescence, as a threat to their freedom to criticize.

∽

Awareness is more effective than any legislative investigation or enactment could hope to be as a deterrent for misuse of governmental powers.

∽

Many of our liberties were purchased by blood upon the field of battle. It was not so in respect to the freedom of the press. This liberty was won for us by attorneys for the defense in prosecutions for criminal libel against courageous publishers who dared to print the truth in respect to those exercising governmental authority.

∽

I maintain the judges ought to have wisdom as well as knowledge. I have been distressed by the willingness of judges to try to punish news-gatherers because they stuck to their code of ethics.

We had a great old judge down in my county when I first started practicing law many years ago when prohibition was the law of the land. They caught one of my clients running a little still—a twenty-gallon copper still. They caught him red-handed. So when they came to the court the prosecutor told me the only thing I could do was plead him guilty and ask the judge to deal with him as gently as possible.

. . . My client was Benton. The prosecutor called

him around to the witness stand and asked him where
he got that still, and Mr. Benton said, "I ain't going
to tell you." He was one of those mountaineers who
had a lot of courage like you displayed. He kept
saying, "Where did you get that still?" and Benton
kept saying, "I ain't going to tell you." Finally the
prosecuting attorney appealed to the judge to make
him tell and the judge said, "Well, Mr. Benton, when
you said you weren't going to tell the prosecuting
attorney where you got the still, I assume you meant
you would rather not tell him," and he said, "That is
right, Judge, but I ain't going to tell him nohow."

Then the prosecutor appealed to the judge to put
Mr. Benton in jail until he told where he got his still,
and I will never forget what the judge said because
it showed he had wisdom as well as knowledge. He
said, "I think everybody needs a code of ethics to get
through this troublesome world," and he said, "It
appears that Mr. Benton has devised himself such a
code. According to his code of ethics, he thinks it is
wrong for him to tell on somebody else." He said, "It
might not be as enlightened a code of ethics as yours
or mine, but I am not going to punish him. I am not
going to send him to jail, because the greatest injury
I can do to any man is to tear down the code of
ethics by which he lives, even though I may not fully
approve of it." So the judge went ahead and gave him
a sentence for the still, but didn't send him to jail for
contempt of court.

I have often thought about those judges sending
newsmen to jail for not disclosing the source of information; if they could exercise a little wisdom like

this judge in North Carolina many years ago, they would be better off.

ⱷ

Inasmuch as the chief objective of freedom of speech and of the press is to secure political freedom for our people and sound government for our land, the press and the broadcast media, as interpreters between the government and the people, have the responsibility to inform the people in respect to public issues.

ⱷ

It is my belief that robust criticism of government by the press and the consequent skepticism of the press on the part of the government are the necessary ingredients of the relationship between the press and the government in a truly free society.

ⱷ

It is essential to the proper administration of justice and particularly to the preservation of fair trial for those charged with crimes that the court be open and that the press be permitted to comment on the courts and the events which transpire in judicial proceedings.

Of course, those of us in public life and those of us who engage in trials sometimes may think that the press goes a little too far, especially when it smites us or our clients.

But my opinion is that the freedom of the press is one of the vital freedoms of our country and we should be very cautious of placing statutory limitations on its exercise.

∽

When the crime is violent, when the emotions of the community cry out for justice, when there is no doubt in the minds of the press and public that the man accused is guilty, it is then most of all that the press must remember, and it is their duty to see that the community remembers, that the defendant is still innocent in the eyes of the law.

∽

Our historic commitment to freedom of the press means that we must tolerate absurd, misleading, and vindictive reports which sometimes appear in newspapers and magazines and on radio and television. It means that thoughts and ideas which we hate and despise will appear in print and be broadcast across the land.

∽

I have an old schoolmate who has notions which are rather peculiar from my viewpoint. He used to send me long documents and ask me to put them in the *Congressional Record*. I disagreed with everything in them and declined to put them in the *Congressional Record*. He said he had a right to forward them and since he was an American citizen and paid taxes, he had a right to require me to put them in the *Congressional Record*.

I told him I had a right to say what I was going to put in the *Congressional Record* because everything

I put in there people attribute to my views. I told him I would get a thousand letters protesting my putting such foolish things in the *Congressional Record* and I refused to put them there.

I think the media ought to have some say in what they will disseminate, and it seems to me it is fundamentally a denial of freedom of speech to tell them they have to publish something that they don't want to publish.

∽

From the moment the type was set on the first printing press, kings and parliaments have attempted to control the press. Public officials have always feared the threat that a free and vigorous press poses to their power and tenure.

∽

Down in Henderson County, we had a very prominent lawyer, a Confederate Colonel Bennett. He was always much distressed when one of his friends passed away, so he used to write a poem about it. They said that Judge Bennett's poems added a new terror to death. I think that the presence of television in the courtroom adds a new terror to the witness and frustrates the search for truth, for which the court is established.

Courts are not established to be circuses or even for the amusement of the public.

∽

Rarely if ever in our history have we actually had to choose between suppression of the press or disaster. In every national war, where security was truly at stake, the press and government found means of accommodating their apparently irreconcilable interests. I see no reason why suppression or censorship is required now if it was not when national survival hung in the balance.

RELIGION

Sam Ervin has a deep, unshakable faith in two documents—the Bible and the Constitution. He appreciates the contribution religion has made to the American ethic and is convinced the nation can derive great strength from its diversity of religious beliefs so long as we maintain the principle that all men of all faiths are free to practice their religion without interference from government.

I look at the universe and behold with wonder the lifegiving sun, which rises in the east at morn, travels across the sky by day, and sets in the west at eventide; the galaxies of stars, which twinkle in the infinite heavens; the clouds, which bring the soil-refreshing rain; the majestic mountains with hills at their knees; the rivers, which water the pleasant valleys and fertile plains, and run endlessly to the sea; the tall trees which lift leafy arms heavenward to pray; the arbutus and dogwood, which brighten

117

springtime, and the marigolds and roses which ornament summer; the glory of the heavens and ripened crops of autumn; the crystal snowflakes, which descend so gently in winter; and the other beautiful things past numbering, which adorn the earth.

I note with awe the order and regularity of the processes of life and nature as the tide ebbs and flows, as the harvest succeeds the seedtime, as the heavenly bodies move in their orbits without mishap in conformity with natural laws. I observe with reverence that, despite the feet of clay on which he makes his earthly rounds, man is endowed with capacity to obey conscience, exercise reason, study holy writings, and aspire to righteous conduct in obedience to spiritual laws.

On the basis of these things, I affirm with complete conviction that the universe and man are not haphazard products of blind atoms wandering aimlessly about in chaos, but, on the contrary, are the creations of God, the Maker of the universe and man.

◌

I covet freedom of religion for all men. Let them study their holy writings and meditate upon their teachings without let or hindrance from government. I cherish this freedom for myself as well as for others.

◌

Political freedom cannot exist in any land where religion controls the state, and religious freedom cannot exist in any land where the state controls religion.

◌

As one ascends the hill which leads to Jefferson's home at Monticello, he passes the burial ground of members of the Jefferson family. He passes the spot where the mortal remains of Thomas Jefferson rest in the tongueless silence of the dreamless dust. On the gravestone of Thomas Jefferson is the epitaph which speaks with as much eloquence as Jefferson used in writing the Declaration of Independence or the Statute of Virginia for Religious Freedom. The statement is as follows:

"Here was buried Thomas Jefferson, author of the Declaration of Independence; the Statute of Virginia for Religious Liberty; and father of the University of Virginia."

At the time that Jefferson decided that these were the words which he wished to have engraved on the stone which marks his last resting place, he had been a member of the Legislature of Virginia; he had been a Governor of the State of Virginia; he had represented Virginia in the Continental Congress; he had served as American Minister to France; he had officiated as Secretary of State in George Washington's Cabinet; he had been twice elected to the highest office within the gift of the American people—the Presidency itself.

Yet, Thomas Jefferson was not concerned that he should be remembered for the high offices which he had filled, but he was concerned that he should be remembered as the author of the Virginia Statute for Religious Freedom, one of the greatest documents ever penned by man. It lays down the proposition that it is sinful and tyrannical to compel a man to

make contributions of money for the propagation of
opinions that he disbelieves.

∽

I see an increasing tendency on the part of churches to want to get their hands in the public till, and
to depend upon tax moneys rather than the volun-
tary contributions of their adherents for support of
their activities. And I think that would be the worst
thing that could happen to this nation.

∽

I might state that I believe that religious instruction is a highly desirable thing, and that any religious
denomination is justified in establishing educational
institutions to make certain that students will receive
instruction in religion as well as in other matters.
But I believe that if the religious denominations wish
to do that they ought to be willing to pay for the cost
of operating these institutions. The institutions are
certainly worthy institutions engaged in a worthwhile
task. And they are undoubtedly doing much of the
Lord's work. But it seems to me that the First
Amendment was clearly designed to prevent the government from taking the taxes of Caesar and giving
them to God or for the furtherance of any of God's
activities.

∽

Sir, what the good Lord can do ought to be constitutional, ought it not?

∽

I think that the greatest book, from a literary as well as from a religious standpoint, ever made available to mankind, is the King James version of the Bible. As soon as my forebears obtained the King James version of the Bible, they adopted it as a guide for their religious faith, and they recorded within its covers their marriages, their births, and their deaths. They found something within that old Book which revealed to them the promises of God, and something which made them fear God and nothing else.

∽

If I understand anything about the Bible, from one end to the other, it teaches freedom.

It says every person has a right to be free. He even has the right to do wrong and to go to Hell instead of going to Heaven if he wants to.

I think certain things should be left to the decision of the individual. If the government is going to undertake to make decisions on what it conceives to be morally right and impose upon us the government's idea of what is morally right, the government is going to destroy our freedom.

∽

I cannot see that there is any harm in a man preferring to go to one church rather than another. Of course, if he is like me and predestined to go to a Presbyterian church, I think he will go there.

∽

The most heart-rending story of history is that of man's struggle against civil and ecclesistical tyranny for the simple right to bow on his own knees before his own God in his own way.

∽

The men and women who gave liberty to America were devout souls. They had learned some of the sorrowful facts of the spiritual life of man in the bitter crucible of experience. Most of them dissented from the doctrines and usages of the churches established by laws in the lands of their origins. They were denied the right to worship God in their own ways. They were compelled to pay tithes for the support and propagation of religious opinions which they disbelieved. They had their marriages annulled and their children adjudged illegitimate for daring to speak their marriage vows before ministers of their own faiths rather than before clergymen of the established churches.

But these cruel oppressions merely steeled their convictions that religion is a private matter between man and his God; that no human authority should undertake to control or interfere with the rights of conscience; and that "to compel a man to furnish contributions of money for the propagation of opinions which he disbelieves is sinful and tyrannical."

For these reasons, our ancestors staked the very existence of America as a free nation upon the principle that all men have a natural and unalienable right to worship Almighty God according to the dictates of their own consciences, and the corollary that this natural and unalienable right can be secured only by keeping the hands of the state out of religion and the hands of religion off the state.

ॐ

I am against allowing government to prescribe thoughts for people. I think religion should undertake to persuade people to have right thoughts, but I do not think government should coerce them to think like government thinks.

ॐ

I would just like to warn my good friend from Minnesota that sometimes these people who undertake to pray wind up suffering disappointment. I have had that personal experience.

I remember when, a few years ago, Senator Dirksen introduced the so-called Dirksen prayer amendment, which as I recall the Senator from Minnesota, the Senator from Indiana, and myself opposed. When the Senator from Illinois [Mr. Dirksen] introduced that proposed amendment, I realized it was highly controversial, and that anyone who interjected himself into that field of endeavor was likely to be misunderstood.

So I got down on my knees and I prayed very fervently that the Dirksen amendment would go away off somewhere into outer space, and not come back to trouble the Senate.

I know I prayed earnestly and I prayed fervently, but my prayers were not answered and that amendment came back here and I had to stand up and face it.

I had always believed in prayer, and I had always

believed that when you prayed fervently your prayers would be answered.

So I took down my Bible to find out why my prayers were not answered in that request, and I found that the Bible does not say simply that fervent prayers will be answered. It says that the fervent prayer of a righteous man availeth much. So I had to draw the conclusion that while I prayed fervently, I was not righteous within the meaning of that verse of the Scripture.

So I just want to warn the Senator from Minnesota to tread very softly in that field, for fear he will suffer a disappointment such as mine.

⟡

If the good Lord had made us so that we could have hindsight in advance, a great many of our errors would be avoided.

⟡

It is impossible to overmagnify the importance of faith in God. It is, in my judgment, the most potent force in the universe. Faith in God gives men and women the strength to face the storms of life and their consequences with the peace which passes understanding. In times of greatest stress, faith in God has the miraculous power to lift ordinary men and women to greatness.

⟡

Religion adds hope to man's desire for immortality. This desire is not to be attributed simply to the egotism of men, or their fear of the unknown beyond the grave, or their repugnance of the thought of their nothingness after death.

The pessimistic philosopher Schopenhauer was sadly in error in his caustic comment that "to desire immortality is to desire the eternal perpetuation of a great mistake." The longing for immortality is prompted by most meritorious motives.

Life on earth at best is all too short and unfinished. Man entertains high hopes for an abundant life with his loved ones, and undertakes worthwhile things for them and his generation. His high hopes vanish as he is robbed of those he loves by death, and his hands drop the working tools of life while his undertakings are incomplete.

As a consequence of these things, our hearts cry out that there must be some place after life's fitful fever is over where tears never flow and rainbows never fade, where high hopes are realized and worthy tasks are accomplished, and where those we "have loved long since and lost awhile" stay with us forever.

I revere religion. I revere religion because it gives us these promises and this hope. I would protect and preserve the right of freedom of religion for all men.

∾

If the good Lord were to put down a requirement to show that we had not committed a single sin for ten years as a prerequisite of salvation, many of us would never see salvation, would we?

∾

Lincoln's disbelief in eternal punishment constituted a reaction to the hellfire sermons he heard in his youth and was based on his conviction that punishment "was intended for the good of the offender" and "must cease when justice is satisfied." He often manifested his disbelief in endless punishment by quoting this paraphrase of Martin Elginbrod's famous epitaph:

> Here lies poor Johnny Kongapod;
> Have mercy on him, Gracious God,
> As he would do if he was God,
> And you were Johnny Kongapod.

ഔ

If the National Council of Churches were to speak to me on a religious subject, I would probably listen to them. But when the National Council of Churches starts talking, as it so often does, about the affairs of Caesar, I do not give very much mind to what it has to say on that subject.

ഔ

I do not claim to be a theologian. I am merely a sinner who looks to the King James version of the Bible for religious guidance.

I find these plain words in First Peter, Chapter Two, verses thirteen to fifteen:

"Submit yourselves to every ordinance of man for the Lord's sake . . . for so is the will of God."

JUDGES, JURIES, AND LAWYERS

Sam Ervin has, on occasion, referred to himself as a "pore country lawyer." Such a self-deprecating characterization is deceptive. While he frequently makes his point by reciting a parable or relating a hill-country lawyer story, he honed his razor-sharp legal mind at Harvard and served with distinction on the Supreme Court of North Carolina. Any adversary who fails to appreciate his knowledge of the law, and of the nature of judges and juries, proceeds at his own peril.

I had occasion, when I had the honor to serve on the Supreme Court of North Carolina, to try to define what is a fair trial. I came to the conclusion that the essence of a fair trial can be defined in this way: In order to have a fair trial, a litigant is entitled to have his cause heard by an unbiased jury, before an impartial judge, in an atmosphere of judicial calm.

The founders of our government were wise men. They knew that tyranny uses the forms of the law to crush those who oppose her will. They knew that the right of trial by jury is the best security of the people against governmental oppression. They knew that the surest test of the credibility of a witness is his confrontation and cross-examination by the adverse party.

෴

Well, if I were asked the question what kind of jury I would like to be tried by, I would like it to depend on one of two things, whether I knew I was guilty or innocent.

If I thought I was innocent, I would like to be tried by the most intelligent jurors I could get. If I thought I was guilty, I would rather be tried by the most unintelligent ones, and the ones most lacking in morality.

෴

I am a great believer in jury trials but I think justice is administered better if you have intelligent rather than unintelligent jurors.

෴

And that is the reason I am in favor of having a system of jury selection like we have in North Carolina. I agree education should not be a qualification. I know a lot of people who have been educated way past their intelligence.

෴

It is highly desirable to get as many citizens as possible to serve on juries. I think it gives a good deal of confidence in the administration of justice on the part of the public generally if they are familiar with it. I think they will come away from the average court persuaded that we have about as fine a system as can be devised to accomplish justice.

ᜇᜎ

As counsel for the defense in cases past numbering, I have urged upon jurors the truism that in the case of doubt it is always better to err on the side of mercy rather than on the side of justice, and on the side of acquittal rather than on the side of conviction.

ᜇᜎ

I remember one case that we had, a notorious case, and when the jury retired, according to the jurors later, one juror asked rather quizzically if it would be a hung jury and the other said, "If we go out there and say 'Not Guilty,' we will really be hung."

ᜇᜎ

One time I was holding court and a man wanted to be excused from the jury panel on the grounds that he was deaf in one ear, and I said, "We will wait to see whether you will be selected to be on a grand jury, because a grand jury hears only one side of a case."

ᜇᜎ

There was a justice of the peace in North Carolina who was trying a civil case between a plaintiff and a defendant. When the plaintiff had produced his evidence and rested his case, the justice of the peace turned to the defendant and said, "I would appreciate it, as a great favor to the court, if you would not offer evidence in this case, because when I hear both sides of the case I have a tendency to become confused, though when I hear only one side I have no difficulty in reaching a decision."

∞

There are eighty-six different Federal Districts in the U.S. and an old lawyer in St. Louis made a speech some time ago in which he said, "Do not waste your time looking up the law in advance, because you can find some Federal District Court decision that will sustain any proposition you make."

∞

My father, who was an active practitioner at the North Carolina Bar for sixty-five years, gave me this sage advice on this point when I entered his law office many years ago: "Salt down the facts; the law will keep."

∞

I am reminded of the old lawyer who was invited to speak to a law school. He said, "I would advise you under no circumstances to ever look up the law before you try the case, because you might find the law is against you, and that will cause you to lose confidence in your case and it is very important for the lawyer to have confidence in his case."

Then one of the students said, "What are you going to do if the other side looks up the law and brings it into court and uses it against you?"

He said, "That is easy. All you have to do is to say to the judge, 'This is bad law and ought to be overruled.' "

∽

As lawyers, we know this: The law requires all laymen to know every bit of the law; it requires lawyers to know a reasonable amount of law; but it does not require judges to know a doggone thing.

∽

I have spent fifteen years of my life judging my fellow travelers to the tomb, and I think I have acquired some capacity to judge matters with what Edmund Burke called the cold neutrality of the impartial judge.

∽

[This] bill, as I interpret it, would remove all Supreme Court Justices from office when they get to be seventy years of age. I don't believe it is bad behavior to get to be seventy years of age. I think the only way you will get to be seventy years of age is to have fairly good behavior.

∽

I don't mind being called "Judge." To me, it is a compliment. But maybe I am in the same fix as a friend of mine in North Carolina who is a doctor and a lawyer both. The doctors call him "Judge" and the lawyers call him "Doctor" and both professions agreed that whenever one of his clients became his patient that he performed a very necessary legal service for him when he drew up his last will and testament.

∽

I had the privilege of serving the North Carolina Supreme Court under a very wise Chief Justice, Walter P. Stacy. The first day I went in the conference room as a member of the court, Judge Stacy said he wanted to explain one rule they had in the conference. He said that in order that the newest member of the court might not feel any necessity for conforming to the views of the oldest members, "We make him express his opinion first as to how a case should be decided, and I want to ask you to follow that rule and frankly state what you think about each case." And he said, "We also have another rule, and that is that nothing which is said in this conference is ever revealed by any members of the conference, and nothing that anyone says is ever made public in any way." He said, "The reason for that is that if you have a good thought or some sound view about the case that is discussed, it will be very helpful; and if you have a fool thought, you don't have to worry about its consequences because it will not be attributed to you outside. And if you have such a fool thought, there is nothing better to do than to

voice it in the presence of friends, so they can swat
it if it deserves to be swatted."

ᕦᕤ

We had a state judge in North Carolina who was
appointed to fill a vacancy and served about five
months. He had one appeal during that five months
and the Supreme Court of North Carolina affirmed
it. Ever after, the judge would brag that during his
entire service on the bench he was only reversed one
time. He made that statement one time in the presence of another judge who told him that if he had
such a sorry record he wouldn't be bragging about it
because all it proved was that he had no more sense
than the Supreme Court of North Carolina and if he
didn't have any more sense than that, he should not
go bragging about it.

ᕦᕤ

. . . I tried my hand at the job for over six years,
trying to write decisions that could not be interpreted
but one way, and I was very discomforted that last
time I walked into a North Carolina court where the
lawyers on both sides were taking a decision I wrote.
One of them said that under this decision certain
evidence was admissible and the other one said that
under this decision the evidence was incompetent. It
is a difficult job, because as Oliver Wendell Holmes
said, a word is not a crystal, transparent and un-
changed; it is the skin of a living thought which may
vary greatly in color and content according to the
circumstances in which it is used.

ᕦᕤ

You and I will pretty much agree that it is a very fortunate thing for us lawyers that we can read the same books and draw different conclusions from them. If that wasn't possible, we would not have near enough lawsuits to keep us all going.

∽

There was a young lawyer who showed up at a revival meeting and was asked to deliver a prayer. Unprepared, he gave a prayer straight from his lawyer's heart: "Stir up much strife amongst the people, Lord," he prayed, "lest thy servant perish."

∽

Now, attorneys may be in low repute in some quarters, but I would say that nobody can get justice in our courts unless he is represented by a competent attorney.

∽

The lawyer plays an indispensable part in a government of laws. He serves justice. Paradoxical as it may seem, he serves justice by serving his clients.

∽

Two North Carolina neighbors, A and B, quarreled about the location of the boundary between their adjoining farms. A said to B, "If you don't concede that my boundary is located where I say, I will bring a suit against you in the Superior Court." B said, "That is all right. I will be there when the case is tried." A said, "If I lose that case in Superior Court, I'll appeal to the Supreme Court of North Carolina."

B said, "All right, I'll be there when that appeal is heard."

Then A said, "If I lose that case in the Supreme Court of North Carolina, I'll appeal to the Supreme Court of the United States."

B said, "That is all right, I'll be there when that appeal is heard."

And then A said, "Well, then if I lose that case in the Supreme Court of the United States, I'll take it straight to Hell."

B said, "I won't be there, but my lawyer will."

∾

The value of the constitutional right to counsel depends greatly on the ability and independence of the attorney who is defending the accused.

∾

The word "epithets" recalls an incident concerning a good old-time lawyer, Mose Harshaw. Mose used to be a lawyer in Caldwell County, which adjoins my county. Sometimes his words became mixed up. Mose had a client who was convicted of assault and battery upon another man, who had applied epithets to him. In begging the court to extend mercy to his client, Mose said, "I hope that in passing sentence on my client upon his conviction of assault and battery, your Honor will bear in mind that he was provoked to do so by the epitaphs hurled at him by the prosecuting witness."

∾

With due respect to all my brethren who differ with me, I do not see how they can very well say that a man is knowingly and willfully acting with a bad purpose when he is merely doing what his lawyer tells him is permissible and legal.

∽

. . . This lawyer down in North Carolina was consulted by the old lady on one occasion who laid a legal problem before him and asked his advice on it, and he gave her his advice and then she arose and started out of the office.

He said, "Wait a minute. You owe me five dollars."

She said, "What for?"

He said, "For my advice."

And she said, "Well I ain't gwine to take it."

∽

Judge David Schenck, a North Carolina lawyer of a bygone generation, was once asked how he justified pleading for a guilty client. His answer merits preservation. He said, "Someday I shall stand before the Bar of Eternal Justice to answer for deeds done by me in the flesh. I shall then have an advocate in the person of Our Lord, who will certainly be pleading for a very guilty client."

∽

I have practiced law for a long time and I have participated in compromises in many cases, never one of any great magnitude, but my experience is that when people settle litigation they do so for approximately the same reason that Hamlet stated in his soliloquy: they are uncertain as to what the courts are going to decide and they take the ills they know of rather than fly to those they do not.

∽

One of the most famous lawyers in Mecklenburg County was Mr. Charles W. Tillett. A young lawyer whom I shall call John Doe brought a suit against the Western Union Telegraph Company, which was one of Mr. Tillett's clients. The young lawyer, John Doe, filed a somewhat vague complaint against the Western Union Telegraph Company, and Mr. Tillett applied to the judge for an order requiring the plaintiff to appear and show cause why he should not make his complaint specific in several respects.

After he issued notice to show cause, the judge happened to meet the plaintiff's lawyer, John Doe, and he said, "John, why don't you go ahead without putting me to the necessity of having a hearing, and amend your complaint in the specific ways in which Mr. Tillett wants it amended?"

Whereupon John Doe said, "Judge, if old man Tillett thinks I am going to tell him what this lawsuit is about, he is a blamed fool."

∽

Federal judges are nearer to monarchs than any other officials in this nation. They are given office for life. They are given a compensation which cannot be decreased during their continuance in office.

There is no power on earth which can keep them within the limits of their constitutional power except Congress, by regulating their jurisdiction.

∽

I have always entertained the notion that when a man goes on the bench that he should read and heed what is set forth above Dante's *Inferno*: "All hope abandon, ye who enter here." I think he should abandon hope of acquiring anything above his salary.

∽

I am inclined to think from my observation that owing to the rareness with which codes of ethics are enforced and owing to the lack of any real sanction, you come down to the point that you are almost compelled to say that it is extremely difficult to establish a code of ethics which will prompt ethical behavior on the part of an unethical man.

∽

I also entertain the belief that ethics ought to be on a higher plane than the law. The law covers everybody.

∽

I have to confess that recent proceedings in the Judiciary Committee and the Senate in respect to nominations to the Supreme Court remind me of an observation I heard a North Carolina lawyer make about 1924. There was a vacancy on the U.S. Circuit Court of Appeals in my circuit and some of the bar suggested that Mr. Tom Rollins of Asheville would make a fine judge of the circuit court. My father, with whom I had practiced, and Mr. Rollins had a case together at that time. My father said to Mr. Rollins, "Tom if you are interested in becoming a circuit judge, I will be glad to get the local bar here to endorse you for the appointment."

Mr. Rollins thanked my father, but said, "I don't care for you to do that. I had a friend down in Alabama that was foolish enough to allow his friends to recommend him for appointment as a Federal Judge. The President hinted he was going to appoint him. The next day this lawyer disappeared, and he has never been heard of since. The only clue they unearthed for his disappearance was the fact that just before he disappeared, he received a telegram: 'All is discovered, flee at once.'"

That would be the course of action I would be tempted to follow if the President should be so foolish as to nominate me for a Federal judgeship.

∞

There was an old country lawyer down in my country that used to interpret the maxim *de minimis lex* by saying, "The law doesn't fish for minnows."

∞

Practicing judges and lawyers of a court of general jurisdiction perform their functions in the workaday world where men and women live, move, and have their being. To them, law is destitute of social value unless it has sufficient stability to afford reliable rules to govern the conduct of people and unless it can be found with reasonable certainty in established legal precedents.

❧

The following story is told in North Carolina: A young lawyer went to an old lawyer for advice as to how to try a lawsuit. The old lawyer said, "If the evidence is against you, talk about the law. If the law is against you, talk about the evidence."

The young lawyer said, "But what do you do when both the evidence and the law are against you?"

"In that event," said the old lawyer, "give somebody hell. That will distract the attention of the judge and the jury from the weakness of your case."

❧

Having done a lot of trial work, and, I might say, always on the side of the accused, I have always wondered about some of our theoretical brethren who insist that there ought to be a right to comment on the failure of a defendant to testify. My experience is that about the first question the jurors ask when they go out to deliberate on the verdict is, "If this fellow wasn't guilty, why didn't he get up there and so state?"

❧

I think about an old member of my bar when I started practicing law, and he always used to say, "I deny the allegation and defy the allegator."

❧

I am afraid of any proposition that undertakes to have controversies settled otherwise than in the courts of law where there are judges who have had to deal with all kinds of problems and are not normally crusaders for any cause other than the cause of justice.

༄

The Founding Fathers left us with a delicate government which if maintained in its proper balance will ensure freedom for generations to come. The vigilance that freedom demands must be provided by each and every citizen—and especially by those of us who know and love the law.

WAR, PEACE, VIETNAM,
AND THE MILITARY

Sam Ervin believes in military preparedness as a deterrent to war and a guarantee of liberty. He views Americans as a people too often inclined to foolishly abandon the security of military strength in pursuit of peace. A twice-wounded and twice-decorated veteran of World War I and a senior member of the Armed Services Committee, he feels wars, if they cannot be avoided, are fought to be won. Thus, he found the American experience in Vietnam profoundly disturbing.

————————

I hate war. But I am compelled to agree with the late Elmer Davis, who said atomic war is bad enough; biological warfare would be worse; but there is one thing worse than either, and that is subjection to an alien oppressor.

࿋

Ever since the Prophet Isaiah predicted that the day would come when swords would be beaten into

143

plowshares and spears into pruning hooks, and the nations would learn war no more, there has been an eager yearning for the arrival of that day. I do not know of anything which history shows prompts Americans in general and American Congresses in particular more to abdicate the exercise of their intellectual functions than this very understandable hunger for peace.

∽

But there seems to be no way in which one can stop the delusion that Congress in some way, by passing a law, can put an end to war, so far as the United States is concerned.

∽

Despite the irrationality of war, mankind has expended a major part of his energy, his time, his treasure, and his blood in waging war. And although our country is a peace-loving nation, every generation of Americans has been compelled to go to war.

∽

Those who decry the high cost of an adequate defense should remember that freedom is not free. It was purchased for us at a great price. If we wish to preserve its blessing for ourselves and our posterity, we must pay the cost of so doing, no matter how great it may be.

∽

We certainly live in the most precarious age that the world has ever known. I remember some years

ago when President Roosevelt first issued a procla-
mation providing, in effect, for two Thanksgiving
Days, one the orthodox Thanksgiving and the other a
Thanksgiving a week earlier. I had an old friend,
Isaac T. Avery, who was a Democratic lawyer in my
home town. I also had a young friend, Russell Berry,
who was a Republican lawyer. The Republican lawyer said to the Democratic lawyer:

"I don't know what you Democrats have done for
the country that requires us to have two Thanksgiv-
ings to thank the good Lord for our blessings."

Mr. Avery, the Democratic lawyer, said to Russell
Berry, the Republican lawyer: "Well, Russell, I
think we might very well find use for two Thanksgiving Days. We can use the first to thank the good
Lord for the Atlantic Ocean and the second to thank
the good Lord for the Pacific Ocean."

Those are blessings for which we might well have
thanked the good Lord in those days, but today the
Atlantic and the Pacific Oceans no longer protect
us because of advanced technology.

⁓

I have always entertained the opinion that when
the politicians or the statesmen—whatever one may
choose to call them—fail in their endeavors to such
an extent that war comes, they ought to take a back
seat and let the generals and the admirals in control
of the armed forces on the scene determine how the
day-to-day tactics of the struggle should be conducted.

⁓

There has never been an army yet that ever won a skirmish when it had 536 or any appreciable number of Commanders-in-Chief. The men who drew the Constitution knew that they could have but one head of the armed forces. And they made the President of the United States that head of the armed forces.

∽

I was told that we were trying to fight a limited war in South Vietnam. Upon being told that, I said, "The trouble with a limited war, being fought in the manner in which this war is being fought, is that those who die in it die in a most unlimited manner."

∽

When I protested this in private, I was asked by the civilian authorities whether I wanted to get us involved in trouble with Red China or Russia. My response to that was that a nation which is reluctant to get its feet wet ought not to cross the Rubicon.

∽

I say with sorrow and, I believe, with truth, that the civilians who had control over our armed forces in Vietnam made it virtually impossible for those boys to win a military victory notwithstanding their valor and their sacrifices.

∽

It was a mistake ever to get involved in the war on the mainland of Asia.

∽

Unfortunately, we cannot repeal history any more than we can repeal the deaths of the more than forty thousand Americans who have died in South Vietnam.

The Creator of this universe made it impossible for us to repeal our mistakes. He does make it possible, however, for us to repent of our mistakes and He gives us an opportunity to minimize the consequences of our mistakes as much as possible.

∽

In connection with the examination of Senator McCarthy, I may say, as an old cross-examiner myself, that I was very much intrigued by something that occurred very early in the cross-examination of General Zwicker, namely, the statement by Senator McCarthy where the Senator made this statement to General Zwicker:

"Don't be coy with me, General."

Now, I rather admired that, in a way. Personally, I would never have been bold enough to have made the observation on a cross-examination of anybody in the military service, unless perhaps, it were a WAVE or a WAC, and I then would have been bold enough to do it only under romantic circumstances, where I was surrounded with soft music, moonlight, and roses; and I am satisfied I never would have been bold enough to give that admonition to either a general or a top sergeant.

∽

Of course, General, there are exceptions to general rules, and any testimony that would indicate to me a total absence of any command influence in any court-martial would be sort of on a par with that old story about the lawyer who was summoned down to the jail to see his client.

The lawyer asked him, "What have they got you here for?"

And the client told him.

The lawyer said, "Well, they can't put you here for that."

And his client said, "Well, I am here."

∽

If the President of the United States determines that new forms of intelligence-gathering activities are necessary to enforce the laws, let him so inform the Congress, and let Congress assign the responsibilities to an appropriate civilian agency.

I suggest the Army regroup and redefine their strategic objectives, lower their sights, and reidentify their enemy. Under our Constitution that enemy is not the American citizen.

∽

I do not think the Army or the Air Force or the Navy are always quite entirely free of that attitude exhibited to me by a juror one time when I was presiding over a first-degree murder trial. They had a special venire summoned in from another county and I asked one of these jurors if he could give him a fair trial. He said, "I think he is guilty of murder in the first degree and he ought to be sent to the gas chamber. I can give him a fair trial."

Now, there are instances of courts-martial in this country that had that attitude and did not hesitate to communicate it.

∽

That reminds me of the old captain who used to read the articles of war to his company and he always failed to distinguish between "and" and "or." Where the article says that a person who commits a certain offense shall be punished so and so or shall suffer such and such, suffer death or such action as the court-martial prescribes, this fellow used to read "suffer death and/or other further punishment as a court-martial might prescribe."

WATERGATE

Now approaching his twilight years, Chairman Sam Ervin is immune to charges of political ambition. He brings to the Watergate hearings a solid reputation for honesty and integrity. His unwavering adherence to fundamental constitutional principles and his long years of experience as a lawyer and a judge serve him well in his tenacious pursuit of truth. He has already entered American folklore as a grandfatherly incarnation of Uncle Sam.

———————

Some have asked what the power and objectives of the Senate Select Committee on Presidential Campaign Activities are. I have never found a finer statement in respect to the desirability and the aim and necessity of Congressional investigations than that made by Richard M. Nixon in relation to his activities as a Congressman holding membership on the Un-American Activities Committee of the House. This statement appears in the chapter entitled "Politics With Honor," in his *Six Crises*.

Despite its vulnerabilities, I strongly believe that the Committee serves several necessary and vital purposes. Woodrow Wilson once said that Congressional investigating committees have three legitimate functions: First, to investigate for the purposes of determining what laws should be enacted. Second, to serve as a watch-dog on the action of the Executive branch of the Government, exposing inefficiency and corruption. Third, and in Wilson's view, probably the most important, to inform the public of great national and international issues."

I would like to add that I consider the investigation being conducted by this Committee most crucial to the welfare of the nation. The Committee, in short, is investigating allegations that men exercising great financial power, great political power, and great governmental power have impaired, if not destroyed, the integrity of the process by which Presidents of the United States are nominated and elected. I do not know anything in which the country could have a greater interest than anything which requires Congress to determine whether or not such conditions existed and whether legislation is necessary to prevent their recurrence at some future date.

∞

If the many allegations made to this date [May, 1973] are true, then the burglars who broke into the headquarters of the Democratic National Committee at the Watergate were in effect breaking into the home of every citizen of the United States. And if these allegations prove to be true, what they were seeking to steal was not the jewels, money, or other property of American citizens, but something much more valuable—their most precious heritage, the right to vote in a free election.

ᔡ

I think that the Watergate tragedy is the greatest tragedy this country has suffered. I used to think that the Civil War was our country's greatest tragedy, but I do remember that there were some redeeming features in the Civil War in that there was some spirit of sacrifice and heroism displayed on both sides. I see no redeeming features in Watergate.

ᔡ

I do not state this in the nature of a threat, but I have been given as Chairman of that Committee a mission to perform and, as often has been said, self-praise is half scandal and I don't know whether this is a derogatory statement about myself, but I would like people to know that I have that quality which one's friends call firmness and one's enemies call obstinacy.

ᔡ

I sort of regret that anything was brought out about the alleged attempt [to discredit me], but I am glad it happened because President Nixon's campaign manager [in North Carolina] in 1968 and again in 1972, Charles R. Jonas, Jr., made this statement, and I cannot refrain from reading it because I am very grateful to him for it.

"I think that Senator Ervin is one of the handful of people in the Senate whom it would be impossible to discredit. I think that is why he was chosen. He has a record of impeccable honesty and integrity. If I had to depend on any one person in the Senate to proceed fairly and in a way that would protect the innocent, it would be Senator Ervin."

I am grateful for that compliment. And further-more, when I was asked about this, I said it did not disturb me at all and, I deeply regret to say, that the indiscretions I had committed were barred by the statute of limitations and lapse of time, and that I had lost my capacity to commit further indiscretions.

SENATOR DANIEL INOUYE: You are not that old.

ᏇᎲᏇ

I've had only two volunteer witnesses in respect to the Watergate. One was Martha Mitchell. But I sort of lost my faith in those telephone calls I re-ceived. In yesterday's edition [of the newspaper], they had a picture of me with a telephone receiver at my ear, and I said, "Martha who?"

Now, the other volunteer witness I have is a preacher. He told me not only was he a preacher, but the Lord had anointed him as the second prophet Elijah. And he said the Lord had told him all about the Watergate. And the Lord had told him to tell me to let him come down as a witness and testify before the Committee. And I told him, I said, "I'd be glad to have the Lord come and testify but I don't believe it would be appropriate for you to come down and tell us what the Lord has told you because somebody might complain that that's hearsay testi-mony."

ᏇᎲᏇ

This is not intimating any criticism at all because I just illustrated myself this morning that my memory is quite fallible, and also the memories of other people are fallible, and the gospel of Matthew, Mark, Luke, and John tell us that when Pontius Pilate, the Roman Governor, ordered the crucifixion of Christ, he wrote out a title and had it put on the Cross. . . . And it is rather significant that the writers of these four gospels disagreed on exactly what this title that was put on the Cross said.

The thirty-seventh verse of the twenty-seventh chapter of Matthew says that the writing which was put on the Cross says: "This is Jesus, the King of the Jews."

The twenty-sixth verse of the fifteenth chapter of Mark has a different version. It says: "The King of the Jews."

The thirty-eighth verse of the twenty-third chapter, Saint Luke, has still a different version of what was on this title, and it says: "This is the King of the Jews."

And then the nineteenth verse of the nineteenth chapter of Saint John has a fourth version of the same words or the same title: "Jesus of Nazareth, the King of the Jews."

And so, I say, if these four good men could have different versions of the same words it is understandable why you and I and other human beings have fallible memories about things sometimes.

∽

The Bible bestows blessings on him who swears to his own word and changeth it not.

∽

Shakespeare asks in one place, "What meat doth this our Caesar eat that he's grown so great?" There's a lot of talk about meat these days. I just wonder what meat these White House aides eat that makes them grow so great.

∽

I think it is very unfortunate for the President of the United States for even the best of motives to undertake to make a request which has the effect of obviating an ordinary feature of the judicial process, that is, the appearance of a witness before a grand jury and affording to the grand jury an opportunity to question the witness.

∽

I hope we don't have to resort to subpoenas, and I am praying very fervently that the good Lord will enter this picture and persuade those who have the power over these witnesses to let them come and we will have a very amicable adjustment of that issue.

I have a friend out in the country who brings me messages he says the Lord gave him to transmit to me, and I told him that in the interest of time I wished he would arrange to have the Lord deliver these messages directly to me, instead of through him as an intermediary, but I have asked him to intercede with the Lord to settle this thing by peaceful means rather than by a confrontation.

∽

I'm not going to let anybody come down like Nico-
demus by night and whisper something in my ear
that the public can't hear.

౸

I am from near Watauga County in North Carolina. This man had been in court over in Boone, the
county seat. He came back that night and was in the
country store and he mentioned the fact that he had
been over to the court in Boone, and somebody
asked him what was going on there.

Well, he said, there was the judge sitting up there,
there was the jury sitting over in the jury box, and
there were the lawyers. He said, some of the lawyers
were objecting and t'others were excepting and the
costs were piling up.

SENATOR HOWARD BAKER: Mr. Chairman, if this
is story-telling time, my distinguished Chairman is
going to have to suffer for having set the example for
me. But in the course of all of our testimony, to the
extent that we have conflicts in it, I am reminded of
an old lawyer in Scott County, Tennessee, named
Haywood Pemberton, who was employed to defend a
man.

He said, "I have just shot a man, Haywood, will
you defend me?"

He said, "Of course, I will defend you. Did you
kill him?"

He said, "No, I have just wounded him."

He said, "That is all right, but just remember, he
will be an awful hard witness again you."

SENATOR DANIEL INOUYE: Mr. Chairman, I regret
I have no Hawaiian stories to tell.

ↄ∕〜

SENATOR ERVIN: In other words, they were holding a fund-raising dinner in the Vice President's hon-
or?

MAURICE STANS: In honor of the Vice President.

SENATOR ERVIN: Yes. And they wanted to make
it appear that they took in fifty thousand dollars
more than they actually took in, didn't they?

MR. STANS: They wanted to make it look more
successful than it apparently was.

SENATOR ERVIN: Yes. In other words, they wanted
to practice a deception on the general public as to
the amount of honor that was paid to the Vice President.

MR. STANS: Mr. Chairman, I am not sure this is
the first time that has happened in American politics.

SENATOR ERVIN: You know, there has been murder and larceny in every generation but that hasn't
made murder meritorious or larceny legal.

ↄ∕〜

I think it would be well for the people in authority
at the White House to consider that nobody ever
made a more fruitless mistake than taking a course
of action which engenders in the minds of the American people, rightly or wrongly, the notion that they
are trying to hide something from the American
people.

ↄ∕〜

I think you have strengthened my faith in the old adage that an honest man is the noblest work of God. I will also meditate for a moment on the old saying: "What a tangled web we weave when first we practice to deceive."

∽

Do you think that men who exercise great political power ought to disregard ethical principles and say they have fulfilled their full duty to the American people as long as they keep on the windy side of the law?

∽

And the only advice you got on the subject was the philosophical observation that "when the going gets tough, the tough get going?"

HUGH W. SLOAN: Yes, sir.

SENATOR ERVIN: Well, that's the sort of enigmatic expression that is worthy of the Sphinx.

∽

I hope that in the future there will be no more demonstrations of any kind and I hope that when people attempt to laugh, anybody in the audience, that they will laugh as inaudibly as possible. I am as mild-mannered a man as ever cut a throat or scuttled a ship and I am going to enforce the rule against demonstrations as fully as I can . . .

∽

I wish you would tell me some way I can keep people from laughing. I have been told the only thing that distinguishes humanity from what humanity, with a lofty attitude of disdain, calls a brute creation, is the fact that man laughs and brute creation does not.

∽

I am going to say, however, that the questions put to Mr. Ehrlichman were rather robust and the answers given by Mr. Ehrlichman in response to those questions sometimes were rather robust, too, and I don't know—I quote the King James version of the Bible and I think that the proverb says that "Merry hearts doeth good like a medicine." And sometimes I think a man personally has a Constitutional right to laugh even in a solemn hearing room.

∽

Well, if you can tell me how to keep a Senator or a Senator's aide from talking, it would be the most miraculous discovery made since the morning stars sang from glory.

∽

My experience around Washington is that if several people get hold of a document, that the thing will more than likely appear in the morning paper—if not telecast that night. I think the protection of information around Washington is about as much as the protection which a sieve affords to the passage of water.

∽

About all you can do in this kind of a situation is to pray the good Lord to give some people the power of restraint, and whether that prayer is answered is dependent on the Lord, not me.

ல

I have always thought that if a political institution or committee enacted the role of an eleemosynary institution it would, like the Pharisee, brag about it on all opportunities, and so you agree with me that Doubting Thomases might think that this money was routed in this clandestine way not only to keep it secret but also to keep these people that were receiving the money secret.

ல

Unfortunately, I wasn't born yesterday and I have observed political organizations a long time and I have never yet seen a political organization which was an eleemosynary institution. But assuming that the Committee to Re-elect the President were an eleemosynary institution, can you tell this committee why it was that when it picked out the objects of its eleemosynary concern that they didn't select anybody except seven men who were accused of complicity in burglarizing the headquarters of the opposition political party?

ல

Now, unfortunately, I do not know whether in California you have lightning bugs, but we have them in North Carolina. Sometimes, I wish that people were not like lightning bugs. Lightning bugs carry their illumination behind them. I would like to ask you if, in retrospect, and with your illumination behind you. . . .

∽

I can't give any retroactive advice to the men who were responsible for this disbursing funds for political purposes and concealing the objectives of the disbursements, but I can suggest to future people who attempt to do that, that when they do, they may be either rightly or wrongly judged by the standards set out in the Scripture where it says: "Men love darkness rather than light because their deeds are evil."

∽

I do not think executive privilege under any circumstances covers wrongdoing. For example, if some Presidential aides decided, under the direction of the President, to set up a counterfeit machine in the White House and use the counterfeit money to pay off the national debt, I think Congress could inquire into that operation.

ATTORNEY GENERAL KLEINDIENST: That may not be a bad idea.

∽

This is a rather remarkable letter about the tapes. If you will notice, the President says he has heard the tapes or some of them, and they sustain his position. But he says he's not going to let anybody else hear them for fear they might draw a different conclusion. . . .

I have very different ideas of separation of powers from those expressed by the President. If such a thing as executive privilege is created by the doctrine of separation of powers, it has these attributes. First, if it exists at all, it only exists in connection with official duties.

Second, under no circumstances can it be invoked on either alleged illegal activities or political campaign activities.

I am certain that the doctrine of separation of powers does not impose upon any President either the duty or the power to undertake to separate a Congressional Committee from access to the truth concerning alleged criminal activities.

ono

If the President had no connection with the so-called Watergate Affair and had no knowledge of the Watergate Affair, there is no basis whatever for the invoking of executive privilege.

ono

I can't resist the temptation to philosophize just a little about the Watergate. The evidence thus far introduced or presented before this Committee tends to show that men upon whom fortune had smiled benevolently and who possessed great financial power, great political power, and great governmental power undertook to nullify the laws of man and the laws of God for the purpose of gaining what history will call a very temporary political advantage.

The evidence also indicates that the efforts to nullify the laws of man might have succeeded if it had not been for a courageous Federal Judge, Judge Sirica, and a very untiring set of investigative reporters. But you come from a state like the State of Mississippi, where they have great faith in the fact that the laws of God are embodied in the King James version of the Bible, and I think that those who participated in this effort to nullify the laws of man and the laws of God overlooked one of the laws of God which is set forth in the seventh verse of the sixth chapter of Galatians: "Be not deceived. God is not mocked; for whatsoever a man soweth, that shall he also reap."

THAT REMINDS ME . . .

Sam Ervin has been called a raconteur, but he is really more in the Southern tradition of Uncle Remus: a storyteller whose stories have a moral. On occasion, he feels it necessary to take the nation upon his knee and speak in parables in order to make his point. His stories do more than just reduce complex subjects to their fundamentals or reduce tensions accompanying the somber business of government. They also reveal his warm humanity and his deep understanding of human motivations and concerns.

Today, I want to discuss an allegation which is becoming more and more frequent: that smoking is all that stands between man and immortality. This proposition is being paraded before the American people with all the pomp and certitude of Madame Curie's discovery of radium.

When I hear these arguments, I am reminded of

a prominent citizen who lived to be ninety-six years of age.

On this ninety-sixth birthday, the newspapers sent their reporters out to interview him. One of them asked: "To what do you attribute your long life?"

The old man replied: "I attribute it to the fact that I have never taken a drink of an alcoholic beverage or smoked a cigarette in all my days."

At that moment, they heard a noise in an adjoining room that sounded like a combined earthquake and cyclone. One of the newspaper reporters said, "Good Lord, what is that?"

The old man said: "That's my old daddy in there on one of his periodic drunks."

෴

Actually, it would be far easier to show statistically that smoking cigarettes prolongs life: First, Americans are living sixteen years longer today than they did in 1920; second, Americans smoke more cigarettes than they did in 1920; and, third, ergo, cigarettes prolong life.

Now, this is not to say tobacco is a health food the equivalent of yogurt. What I am saying is that, from such logic as this, no valid conclusions can be drawn.

෴

If we want to be perfectly realistic and reduce the number of people dying from lung cancer, since it is a disease of the aging, we are going to have to arrange some way to kill off people earlier in life before they reach the age at which lung cancer has its highest incidence.

∾

It seems to me sometimes that the cure is worse than the disease. You can cure a man's headache by shooting him through the head with a high powered revolver. That will cure the headache, but destroy the man.

∾

Ironically, the factories that bring good jobs to my mountain constituents pollute the streams and drive away the tourists—another lucrative industry in those parts. Moreover, these industries deprive those who live a few miles downstream of decent drinking water. In fact, it has been rumored that the situation once became so bad that the fellows downstream had to devise ingenious ways of distilling their water and, oddly enough, the result was mountain dew.

∾

South Carolina has always excelled in all respects, in the character of its Senators and also in the character of the liars it has produced.

In Darlington County, they had one of the most gifted liars, who was known as Huckleberry Hart. He could tell a magnificent lie on any occasion, with the slightest opportunity or provocation. One day he was driving along the road, and one of his friends met him and said: "Huckleberry, tell us a lie."

He said, "I will not do it, I haven't got time. And

besides the Pee Dee River is on fire and I have got
to put it out."

That was before rivers became fire hazards and
while the rivers of South Carolina were still pure
streams.

ᗧᗣ

In my county we have an area called the South
Mountains. One of the South Mountaineers had
been buying groceries on credit. He went to the
grocery store to pay his bill. When the grocer ad-
vised him as to the amount of the bill, the South
Mountaineer started to complain because he thought
the amount named exceeded what was actually due.
The grocer took his account books and laid them
on the counter in front of the South Mountaineer
and said, "Here are the figures. You know figures
don't lie."

The South Mountaineer said, "I know that figures
don't lie, but liars sure do figure."

Liars are not the only people who figure. Even
honest men sometimes engage in this activity. When
honest men are determined to persuade people by
propaganda that they have the only righteous views
in connection with a problem, they are inclined to
ignore, or forget figures which militate against their
position.

ᗧᗣ

WITNESS: Senator, I am just giving the figures.
SENATOR ERVIN: That is what the storekeeper
was giving the old mountaineer.

ᗧᗣ

A pioneer North Carolina couple went to town in their covered wagon to do their fall shopping. When they got back home, Mary was checking over the shopkeeper's list of their purchases.

"That merchant," she said, "is crooked. He charged us for a lot of stuff we didn't get. Just look here: so many yards of calico, so much; ditto, so much; so many yards of gingham, so much; ditto, so much. We never bought any ditto."

John got on his horse and rushed back to town. When he got back, Mary ran out and asked: "What did you find out?"

"I found out," said John, "that I'm a fool and you are a 'ditto.'"

∽

Let me explain what a billion dollars is. If a husband should give his wife a billion dollars on the understanding that she would spend a thousand dollars of it every day except the extra day in leap year and would not return until all was spent, it would be 2,739 years, two months, and five days before he would see her again.

∽

The most temporary thing in existence is the debt limit.

∽

Now we enjoy so much the exercise of setting fictitious, India-rubber, expanding debt limits that we raise it two or three times a year. It has become

a favorite legislative exercise in what I call a species
of legislative gymnastics.

ᜣᜥᜣ

The Senator from North Carolina submits that
the administration wants a higher springboard so it
can dive deeper into the sea of fiscal irresponsibility.

ᜣᜥᜣ

In my book, a jimson weed smells just as rank,
regardless of what name one gives it. It does not keep
deficit spending from being deficit spending by calling it a full-employment budget.

It is just like the unified budget we have. It is
just something to hide government iniquity from
people who are susceptible to being deceived.

ᜣᜥᜣ

Deficit spending is dishonest in purpose and ruin-
ous in practice. It undertakes to transfer to the
future the burdens of the present. In so doing, it
robs the past of its savings, the future of its earn-
ings, and both the present and the future of their
economic strength.

ᜣᜥᜣ

The Senator from North Carolina has always believed that the Federal government should have
enough courage and enough intelligence to cut its
expenditures so that they will not exceed its income
by taxation so that its income will cover its expenditures.

ᜣᜥᜣ

The Senator from North Carolina has voted against every proposal made since he came to the Senate to reduce Federal taxes, because the Senator from North Carolina believes in the principle of honesty embodied in the assertion that an individual or a government ought to be just before it is generous.

∾

To be sure, government acts in an anti-inflationary way when it collects taxes and applies them to its debts. But it is illogical to maintain that it is inflationary for the people to spend their money as they please, and anti-inflationary for the government to take the people's money from them and spend it as the government pleases.

∾

If the President and the Congress want to give any new sums to the states and cities, they ought to exercise the political courage to insist that old taxes be raised or new taxes be imposed sufficient to cover the cost of the program. Anyone who expects that to happen is about as foolish as King Canute, who commanded the ocean waves to be still.

∾

In my young days we had a rash of serious failures sometimes in baseball. I used to play sandlot baseball and it was all we could do as kids to raise enough money to buy a dollar-and-a-quarter baseball, and sometimes [we] knocked the baseball into the honeysuckle vines and lost it and we had to call the game. In those days, Joe Jackson was playing on a textile-plant team down in Greenville, South Carolina, and he was a left-handed hitter and he had an awful clout. He hit the ball deep into right field every time he came to bat. There was a big swamp in the right field and he knocked the baseball into that swamp and they fired him from the team because he was too much of an expense to them.

∽

I've lost the chlorophyll out of my hair, and I think that youth is the most wonderful thing in the world and I think it's a pity the Lord has to waste it all on young people. I think he ought to give people of my vintage a little part of it.

∽

When I consider the urgency of this problem, I am reminded of the experience of an elderly couple, Mattie and Jed, who lived in the South Mountains of North Carolina. Mattie's uncle died and left her some money. She decided to spend it on the one thing she wanted most in the world, a grandfather clock. So they went to town, selected a clock with the loudest chimes they could find, and carried it back to the house in a pickup truck.

They were so delighted with the chimes that they sat up all the first night just listening to them. Then they took turns sitting up. The third night, it was Jed's turn to listen, and as he was dozing in his rocking chair, the clock struck midnight. He listened sleepily as the chimes tolled ten, eleven, twelve, then jumped wide-eyed as they continued to strike one, two, three, and on. He ran to his wife, calling "Mattie! Wake up! It's later than it's done ever been before!"

∽

Anxiety causes one concern about future events likely to occur and induces him to take provident steps to prepare for them, whereas fear fills one with dread of dangers which are imaginary or dangers which cannot be avoided.

∽

Age has many difficult handicaps, but I think the only way you get wisdom is through experience, and you can't have very much experience when you're very young.

∽

I don't think I've changed. I may have gotten a little more pronounced in some of my views . . . but I've always felt that the most precious value of civilization is the freedom of the individual.

I've always felt that the individual should have as much freedom as possible, as much as government can give him, without jeopardizing the rights of other people.

∽

We will not fool history as we fool ourselves when we steal freedom from one man to confer it on another. The preservation of liberty is tedious work, and we must not be distracted from it by the civil-rights sideshow which robs us in its own name's sake.

ↄﾉﾟ

We had a man down in my state that did not agree with anybody about anything. He found that cabbage didn't agree with him, and thereafter he wouldn't eat anything but cabbage.

ↄﾉﾟ

You can make a very good case for the proposition that if you want to engage in logic as to the powers of the government to do what is best for the people, the government should have the power to prescribe what the people will eat or what their diet should be in the interest of keeping them from overeating.

ↄﾉﾟ

I have always been able to sympathize with what Jonah is reputed to have said after the whale threw him off on dry land after three days:
"If you'd kept your mouth shut, this thing wouldn't have happened."

ↄﾉﾟ

I do not know exactly what domestic subversion is, except I have noticed that people who use that

term a great deal usually apply it to the people who
happen to disagree with them on fundamental matters.

∽

They used to tell me that education was like a
grindstone; it sharpened one's intelligence.

Beard!

∽

One of the most famous educators of Burke
County and surrounding portions of North Carolina was Robert Logon Patton, commonly called
"Logue." Mr. Patton began his teaching career in
Jonas Ridge, a portion of Burke County situated in
the mountains. He taught in a neighborhood school
and lived in a nearby mountain cabin where he
shared the room of the old grandfather of the house
who wore an extremely long beard. One night sitting
before the fire, Mr. Patton asked the old mountaineer, for want of other conversation, what he did
with his beard when he slept.

"Do you put it under the cover, or do you leave it
out of the cover?"

"I have had this beard for more than fifty years,
and I have never thought of that before," the
mountaineer said.

Mr. Patton said that on that same night, at some
small hour of the night, he was awakened by the
old mountaineer walking to and fro. Mr. Patton
asked him whether he was sick. He replied, "No,
it's that fool question you asked me last night that
got me up. I put my beard under the cover and I

couldn't sleep. Then I left it out and that didn't feel natural, and I couldn't sleep. I wish you hadn't asked me that fool question."

ᔙ

Human nature is sometimes a rather hard thing to determine. I have always thought of the old story about the minister down on the farm. A member of the church stopped by and saw him working in a field, and he said, "John, you and the Lord have certainly done a wonderful thing with this farm." And the preacher said, "You ought to have seen the farm when the Lord was running it by himself."

ᔙ

The current increase in property values is because of the simple fact that the good Lord is making no more land, but he is making a whole lot more people.

ᔙ

This reminds me of a story that happened up in the mountains of Watauga County. The people up there are hardworking and Godfearing, so they often have revival services in the churches several times a year. One particular preacher, who was holding a revival meeting one night, asked, at the end of the service, for all the sinners to come up to the altar and repent. This one old farmer, being the habitual repenter that he was, slowly arose from the pew to make this yearly pilgrimage toward the altar. As he neared the front of the little country church, he raised his voice aloud and sung, "Lord, fill me, fill me!"

The wise old preacher lifted his hands toward the heavens and said, "Yes, Lord, fill him, fill him good. He leaks!"